This book is robust with fresh, hands-on, practical actions that will give anyone serious about having impact for DEI efforts and investment ready-to-implement, productive strategies and tactics to effectively address evidence-based behaviors in workplace organizations that will have sustaining power.

—Barbara Nobles Crawford, PhD
CEO, Nobles Crawford & Partners
Former organization behavior and development
consultant, Harvard University

In a time of judicial and corporate confusion over diversity, equity, and inclusion, Sandra Upton brings clear guidance based on decades of experience in the field. Following her lead, any well-intended organization can achieve worthy goals. Over the many years I've known Upton, she's always been a solid scholar, an unsurpassed consultant, and an author of prudence, charity, and grace. In *Make It Last*, she breathes new life into DEI—exactly the gift we need at exactly the time it's needed.

—A. James Heynen
Senior managing partner, RTM LTD.

Many organizations are saying they are committed to DEI, but few have a real strategy. Not only does this book help organizations develop a roadmap for the work, but it also teaches them how to operationalize it.

—Deepa Purushothamn
Best-Selling author, *The First, the Few, The Only*

Reading through the details of *Make It Last: A Roadmap and Practical Strategies for How to Do DEI Work* by Sandra Upton, I can't help but feel a surge of excitement. As someone deeply engaged in the DEI space, the author's dedication to equipping leaders with actionable strategies truly resonated with me. The blend of John Kotter's change management framework and Sandra Upton's twenty-five-plus years of DEI expertise seems like a recipe for success, promising to guide us toward creating lasting and impactful change. The inclusion of seasoned professionals adds a genuine touch, making this book a potential companion for anyone committed to driving real transformation in the realm of diversity, equity, and inclusion.

—Lori Spicer-Robertson
Chief diversity officer, St. Jude Children's
Research Hospital
Founder, The DEI Collective

Make It Last is a comprehensive and practical guide about how DEI initiatives can succeed and be sustainable. Dr. Sandra Upton has combined her extensive experience and best practices in the field to create a powerful and compelling roadmap for implementing DEI efforts. It should be a must read for CEOs and corporations alike committed to DEI but not satisfied with previous results.

—David A. Thomas, PhD
President, Morehouse College
Professor Emeritus, Harvard Business School

Very few leaders bring academic validity, experience, and storytelling together in such a compelling way as Dr. Sandra Upton does. She is passionately committed to the hard and uncomfortable work required to see through the change that workplaces so desperately need. She shares her knowledge, learning, and experiences in an extremely succinct way through her book, along with some very practical ways organizations can truly propel their DEI work to make it meaningful, lasting, and impactful.

—Ritika Wadhwa, CEO and founder,
Prabhaav Global

MAKE IT LAST

MAKE IT LAST

Dr. Sandra Upton

Make It Last: A Roadmap and Practical Strategies for How to Do DEI Work by Sandra Upton

Published by Upton Consulting Group in partnership with Embolden Media Group
1407 Laurel Ave, Grand Rapids, Michigan 49506
www.UptonConsultingGroup.com

Visit the author's website at www.uptonconsultinggroup.com
International Standard Book Number: 978-1-7352282-9-7

While the author has made every effort to provide accurate internet addresses at the time of publication, neither the publisher nor the author assumes any responsibility for errors or for changes that occur after publication. Further, the publisher does not have any control over and does not assume any responsibility for author or third-party websites or their content.

24 25 26 27 28 — 9 8 7 6 5 4 3 2 1
Printed in the United States of America

For my family—Robert, Alexis, Devin, Deon, and Mom. You are my world, my top priority, and the reason I do what I do.

To my sweet grandmother, Maude Moss— I dedicate this book to you. Your faith, strength, love, and kindness toward everyone, regardless of their cultural background, laid the blueprint for how I try to live out my life and God-given purpose. Although you are no longer here on this earth, you are in my heart and with me every single day.

Today our very survival depends on our ability to stay awake, to adjust to new ideas, to remain vigilant, and to face the challenge of change.

—MARTIN LUTHER KING, JR.

CONTENTS

Foreword

G IVEN RECENT AFFIRMATIVE action decisions by the Supreme Court of the United States (SCOTUS), coupled with its current makeup, as well as the nationwide state legislative attacks on laws, policies, and programs to uphold this country's founding promises of equality for all that seek the comfort of our shores, the urge to scream for "Diversity, Equity, and Inclusion" (DEI) is strong, and to say "If not now, when?" supported by "Now, more than ever."

I fear that American corporations and businesses responses to SCOTUS' decisions could lead to more and more adverse actions against employees of color. While those employees will want to challenge those actions, it seems inevitable that future SCOTUS decisions may attempt to invalidate other federal (and state) laws, such as Title VI, Title VII, and even Title IX. Although the Court did not address every similar and related law in their recent rulings, the alarming and lurking danger looming behind the recent rulings is the trickle-down effect of the principles contained in the decisions. Today, it begins with race in education. It could end in the abolishment of every law that offers a scintilla of protection to any American citizen who belongs to a protected class. However, our country is better because of laws that serve to prohibit unlawful misconduct and treatment in employment and education. We should all be concerned and fight against the concerted effort to rewrite and overrule hard-fought civil rights laws that protect American citizens from illegal discrimination, harassment, and retaliation on the basis of race and color.

If universities are not proactive in redesigning their recruitment efforts, one obvious and predictable outcome of the recent decision is that diverse enrollment in universities across the country will decline. The traditional employer talent pipelines established through higher education institutions are also likely to be affected in the next decade due to this ruling. In the amicus briefings filed in the Harvard and North Carolina cases, it was clear that most companies want a diverse workforce since their products are consumed by growing diverse customer bases, and it is ultimately in their best economic interest to retain employees who reflect those bases. In my opinion, in the absence of affirmative action programs, DEI programs can make a significant difference as we move forward.

Hiring and retention efforts that incorporate DEI principles and are intentionally targeted and designed to expand the pool of qualified candidates will foster a work environment where people of all backgrounds feel comfortable and have a sense of belonging. This undoubtedly increases the chance of enhancing both the work environment and the quality of the work being done. And certainly, choosing and crafting the language used in communications to employees and candidates about DEI initiatives will be of the utmost importance to preempt the potential expected legal challenges (*e.g.*, reverse discrimination, etc.) that will continue to arise against DEI efforts in the workplace. But there is no need to become fearful. Worst yet, organizations should not shrink back on their DEI efforts. We can rise above these challenges.

Now, more than ever, this book, *Make It Last: A Roadmap and Practical Strategies for How to Do DEI Work*, is a necessary and welcomed read. DEI principles and strategies were informed and molded by every civil rights law passed in this country. I urge everyone who is able to take action and do the necessary work to preserve the legacy of civil rights laws in America and create and implement strategies that will continue to move DEI forward.

—STEPHEN R. DREW

NATIONAL CIVIL RIGHTS AND EMPLOYMENT LAW ATTORNEY

Preface

A S SOMEONE WHO taught and worked in academia for nearly eighteen years, I place a high value on research. I also believe difficult conversations are easier to have when indisputable facts are accepted by all. In the world of diversity, equity, and inclusion (DEI), solid research supports the value and benefits of creating diverse, equitable, and inclusive workplaces. We know that when organizations and leaders use culturally intelligent strategies to attract, retain, and empower a diverse team of employees, not only does it positively impact the bottom line, but everyone wins. We have the data. It's not a zero-sum game.

While research-based theories and frameworks don't always show us how to get the work done, they are critical for helping us think about ways to frame the conversation, and adjust our mindset. The goal of this book is to get to the *how*. It's designed to equip DEI leaders and allies with real strategies for accomplishing the work and experiencing long-term and impactful results.

DEI AND CHANGE MANAGEMENT

To start, we must have a clear understanding of the relationship between DEI and change management.

In a 2017 *Harvard Business Review* article titled "All Management Is Change Management,"[1] Robert H. Schaffer wrote, "Leaders should view change not as an occasional disruptor but as the very essence of the management job." Leading with DEI work is no exception. At the end of the day, DEI is all about change management—changing individual behaviors and systems.

Yet 70 percent of large-scale organizational change efforts fail. John Kotter, Harvard Business School professor and renowned change management expert, created the 8-Step Model of Change, outlined in his book *Leading Change*.[2] For the last forty years, this model has been viewed as one of the most adopted management models across the globe. It was developed based on the extensive research of hundreds of organizations going through the process of change. Kotter's research revealed that only 30 percent of change efforts succeed, largely because those leading the efforts neglected important steps. If DEI is about changing individual behaviors and systems, then applying a research-based, chronological framework to the process significantly improves the DEI leader's and organization's ability to change. Developing and following a strategic DEI roadmap also increases an organization's chance of transforming into a diverse and inclusive organization that is both authentic and sustainable.

With a strategic framework in place, organizations are less likely to default on delivering results. Utilizing a change management framework minimizes the likelihood of organizations abandoning the efforts altogether. Moving your DEI efforts from performative to operational using a change management framework is how we will get the work done and make it last.

In this book, I have adapted Kotter's change management framework and enhanced it with my expertise and DEI best practices to create a foundation for our work together. The result is a guide for how to create and implement a DEI strategic roadmap for your organization. I have contextualized the framework of change to deliver effective DEI outcomes. You'll need to do the same as you consider the framework and strategies within the context of your organization or department and your DEI journey.

Introduction

I T'S A FAMILIAR and painful story. A new client will come to me and say, "Our entire team went through an intensive diversity, equity, and inclusion certificate program at a prominent university. The theories and content were helpful, and we learned a lot. But we came back to our organization still having little to no clue how to actually do the work!"

Good intentions falter when they need to become actual strategies.

This book came about because I hear these sentiments from DEI leaders and allies across departments, industries, and the world. Given the ups and downs of the role of chief diversity officers (CDOs), even after George Floyd's murder in the spring of 2020, most of us working in the DEI space are distressingly aware of how much work remains undone. A review of what has—and hasn't—changed about being a chief diversity officer in a 2022 *Harvard Business Review* piece captured interview findings of more than forty CDOs.[1] The testimony they offered? Within their organizations, much has been promised, but little has been delivered. A "Future of Diversity, Equity, and Inclusion 2022" study by HR.com[2] echoed parallel findings based on interviews of more than 367 human resource leaders from across the globe.

The fact is most of today's organizations lack mature and effective DEI efforts. It's troubling that 80 percent of organizations were found to be "going through the motions."[3] And that's not even considering the intense amount of external resistance, backlash, and polarization that exists in our culture toward this DEI work.

Despite these dismal reports and realities, it isn't all doom and gloom. We've made progress. We've generally done well at teaching the *what* of DEI and even the *why*. Where we've most frequently tripped and fallen short is the *how*. DEI leaders and allies have lacked proven, effective strategies for how to do the work. It's easy—and even important—to talk about the need for DEI. But talk will do no good long term unless we have a solid grasp of what we must do and how we must do it. How do we operationalize our good intentions and high hopes? Answering this question is the key to the DEI kingdom.

After nearly three decades of engaging in DEI work, I have files of notes and a network of valued relationships proving the pattern. My work and learning with hundreds of organizations around the globe continually remind me how hungry DEI practitioners are for clear, proven, and substantive guidance.

Dedicated DEI leaders and allies want practical strategies for successfully accomplishing the work. What's more, such strategies are known. The map has been drawn. Failure to recognize and use these strategies is a tragic legacy. We must—and we can—transform feelings of failure and frustration into realities of success when it comes to DEI.

My DEI Journey

My early experience with DEI came through five years of working as a consultant at a boutique management consulting firm. We were a small company with a large, influential footprint, especially in the corporate world. I was young and learning a lot. I was also trying to navigate my own lived experiences as a twenty-something Black woman in corporate America.

I recall experiencing several microaggressions and different forms of discrimination early in my career, including the executive who said plainly, "If you don't sound white, you can't work here." I remember trying to fit into the dominant culture and being fearful of bringing my authentic self to work. To be completely honest, it took me years to break out of this toxic mindset, to feel free to do and be me.

As my own personal and professional journey unfolded, I was able to observe firsthand the challenges our partners had committing to and creating diverse and inclusive workplaces. They were all over the map and at various stages of the work. Some were committed to it. Others offered lip service to the ideals, but their efforts were largely performative. And some, frankly, could hardly have cared less; they were eager to get back to business as usual. Even in the early days of my career, and even when my role was not specifically one of consulting them on their DEI efforts, or lack thereof, I saw how many organizations were struggling and needed guidance.

My first formal role as a strategic leader in this work was when I served as part of the DEI Council at the university where I was employed. I came in as a faculty member, and eventually, I was made dean of the School of Business. Among the values I brought with me was a deep concern for diversity, equity, and inclusion. I wanted help to make our campus community more diverse and inclusive. When the invitation to join the council arrived, I immediately said yes.

My council colleagues and I were a diverse team of passionate leaders from across the university who, individually and collectively, cared deeply about DEI. Yet none of us was an expert in this space. We had no budget, little decision-making authority, and limited influence with top leadership. As a consequence, and like so many other DEI efforts, we were part of the 70 percent of change efforts that fail.

What do I think caused us to fail? For starters, we didn't have a strategy. And while our efforts weren't performative, they were still activity-based versus outcome-driven. This, combined with the other challenges, kept us in the 70 percent.

This early experience doesn't prove DEI councils don't work. In fact, it's just the opposite. If formed properly and well resourced, DEI councils can be an incredibly valuable part of DEI work. In fact, one of the first actions many organizations take to launch their DEI efforts is to form a DEI council. The problem is that appointing that council is often both the first and last action they take. They get stuck at the point of merely forming the group.

This is exactly why I have written this book. Someone needs to provide strategic leadership for the work and its forward progress in an organization. Ideally, this person will be a CDO with decision-making power, influence, a budget, and resources to successfully move the work forward. But even with a gifted CDO, and regardless of the stage your organization may be on the journey, one thing is clear: DEI work requires everyone to be involved. To be successful, it demands shared responsibility across the organization for understanding and implementing the strategies.

Is This Book for You?

I've come a long way from serving as a DEI council member. And my three decades of work in this space confirm that I am in this work for the long run. What about you?

Think about your current role in relation to DEI. Are you an experienced DEI practitioner? Are you new to the work with enough fear of failure to feel paralyzed? Perhaps you are somewhere in between. Wherever you are on the continuum, there's something in these pages for you.

Whether you are a CDO, part of a DEI council, the leader of an employee resource group, a human resource business partner, the head of marketing, the director of admissions at a university, or a program manager at a non-profit—if you consider yourself a DEI ally and are committed to helping this work move forward in your organization, this book is for you.

Rookie or veteran, full of fresh hope or feeling worn down by your previous attempts, whether you just accepted a role this week or have been working in this space since before the work had a name—wherever you are between these extremes, this book is for you too.

Who Does What?

As we embark on this shared journey to operationalize DEI work, I want to unpack what I mean by DEI strategic leaders and allies. We hear these labels tossed around in the space, but they often mean different things to different people in different settings.

Strategic leaders are those who operate in a clearly defined leadership role directly tied to diversity. It could be a chief diversity officer, diversity manager, or chief human resources officer. And let me hasten to say, I acknowledge the debate about whether DEI should fall under human resources. Some argue that DEI should be its own business function. When placed under HR, it can suggest that no one outside of HR is responsible for the work. Some also argue that the function of

HR isn't always in the best interest of DEI work. These are fair arguments with legitimate concerns. DEI should not be seen as just an HR strategy. It's a business strategy and should impact every business function across the organization. However, I've seen it live under HR, and if the assumptions noted here are considered and addressed properly, it can work.

Allies, on the other hand, are individuals who intentionally and actively promote equity and opportunities for others. They operate through acts of advocacy and efforts to influence systemic change, particularly for underrepresented groups. For example, if they see unfair bias toward certain underrepresented groups in the hiring process, they fight to remove it. If they are in an influential leadership role, they help to level the playing field by helping to ensure pay equity. Or if they are on the front lines and witness a microaggression toward a person of color, a woman, or anyone from any other marginalized group, they speak up on behalf of that person.

Now, you may be both a strategic leader and an ally. Or you may be one or the other. Both require a serious commitment—more than what many think or are willing to actually do. According to the "State of Allyship-in-Action Benchmark Study," men viewed other men as allies at work two times more than woman viewed them.[4] The Allyship Continuum developed within this study, although originally designed to consider how men are allies for women, is a great tool to assess where you are as an ally with any underrepresented or historically excluded group.

THE ALLYSHIP CONTINUUM[5]

Advocate	Visible in supporting underrepresented groups and encouraging others to do the same; they make intentional choices and actions to advance underrepresented groups in the workplace.
Active	Well-informed and willing to engage underrepresented groups; as supporters they are observing, sharing, and learning to influence others.
Aware	Express some interest and/or desire to engage underrepresented groups in the workplace and are in the process of learning and observing.
Ambivalent	May not realize they are hindering equity in the workplace; may be indifferent to the concept of allyship.
Anti	Actively work against underrepresented groups in the workplace, degrading and devaluing them on a regular basis.

So, where on the continuum are you? If you're committed to reading this book, it's highly unlikely you're an "anti-ally." But are you an unshakeable, rock-solid, no-one-can-dissuade-you advocate? To make organizations truly diverse, equitable, and inclusive, that's the kind of support we need—and this book will unlock the secrets that show you how to do it.

What Keeps You Up at Night?

By now you've probably figured out where you land on the Allyship Continuum. You may even be comfortable with your position. That's great! But as we know, DEI work isn't as simple as tracking yourself on a single-dimensional chart. Diversity, equity, and inclusion is nuanced. The work is too. We all come to it with different challenges, levels of experience, and comfort. Yet the challenges we face share common threads and fears. So before we continue, let's see what keeps you up at night when it comes to this work.

Some of the challenges I hear related to this are quite common:

- "I'm passionate about the work, but I'm not an expert in DEI."

- "I have to do my full-time job *plus* the DEI work. There's not enough time."

- "I'm afraid I'll say or do the wrong thing."

- "I have no influence or decision-making authority in my organization."

- "This work feels overwhelming. I don't even know where to start."

In addition, one of the biggest concerns underrepresented groups have is the frustration of being misinterpreted or labeled, especially when speaking about issues related to DEI. In her book *I'm Not Yelling*, Elizabeth Leiba talks about the pushback African American women face in corporate America when speaking their truths and challenging the systems that have held Black women back. Leiba describes these as attempts by the dominant culture to police tone and stop Black women from being their authentic selves.

As an African American woman myself, I can personally relate. At a previous employer, I was part of the senior leadership team. I recall being in a meeting with other leaders, who happened to be all white. Although I can't remember the topic of discussion on this particular day, one of the women in the room, who was white, made a statement I didn't agree with.

Typically in a situation like this, if I didn't agree with something, I would express my concern but back off if I got significant pushback, especially by other senior leaders.

Not this time. This time, I felt too strongly about my opinion. So I said, "I don't agree. Can we talk about this a bit more?"

The woman's response was to say, "Sandra, I'm not going to argue with you!"

"Who's arguing?" I asked. "Just because I don't agree with this decision and I'd like to discuss it further doesn't mean I'm arguing."

That response didn't sit well with her, and I didn't get much support in front of the other leaders in the room.

This was one of several moments where I was reminded that as long as I went along and didn't challenge others or the systems, I would be accepted. Any resistance on my part, regardless of how polite I tried to be about it, risked my being perceived as argumentative, angry, or difficult.

These scenarios are real for many women of color and other historically marginalized groups. It's important to acknowledge these challenges are important and must be part of the conversation and work, even if it's uncomfortable. But here's something that might help; research confirms that when we seek discomfort as a signal of growth, it can increase our motivation and performance.[6]

No matter what keeps you up at night when it comes to DEI work, know that we're all in this together. DEI is a shared journey. We never arrive at a place of DEI perfection; we simply make progress. We do this by honoring the truth about our current state and committing to do the hard and often uncomfortable work of making things better for everyone, especially those who are underrepresented or who have been disadvantaged. The truth is we have a long road ahead, but we do not have to go it alone. If we work together, our collective momentum will propel us forward on the DEI journey.

It can happen. Listen to what happened with one of my clients who was new to his role as a DEI manager. He was terrified of not being taken seriously by leadership and others across the organization. He feared not having enough social capital or influence to make any progress in the work. But over a six-month period, I helped him develop a strategic roadmap for his organization. When we finished, it was clear much work needed to be done—but now he had a roadmap built from quality data, solid metrics, realistic goals, and realistic timelines. He also understood it would take more than just him doing the work. He knew it would be a journey for everyone involved. During the planning process, his confidence and commitment to the work soared by leaps and bounds. When I checked in with him a few months later, the organization was already seeing outcome-based results.

Like my client, soon what's keeping you up will become a thing of the past, becoming what *kept* you up. Let's look at how you can get there.

RULES OF ENGAGEMENT

As we embark on this DEI journey, I want to suggest a few ground rules. These rules of engagement will allow you to work progressively from a defined starting place. They will also help you remain engaged, especially when you are tempted to tap out or give up.

Rule #1: Develop a strategy to protect your mental health.

Diversity and compassion fatigue is real. Chief diversity officers and others leading this work are more exhausted than ever. Before we jump into developing a DEI strategy for your organization, you need to develop a strategy to protect your mental health.

You want to be mindful of your mental state while at and outside of work. This work can be heavy. It can be draining. Depending on the various factors and nuances in place in your situation, it can be quite exhausting physically too.

A 2022 study on workforce mental health conducted by Lyra,[7] a leading behavioral health company, indicates overall anxiety and stress levels continue to increase in the United States. The research reveals we are more depressed, burned out, and impacted by mental health than ever. Their breakdown also provides clear statistics on how mental health has impacted the ability to work by generation. (My experience in other nations has convinced me this is likely the case in other parts of the world as well.) The bottom line is if you aren't careful and intentional about creating space to safeguard your mental health—not just in this work but overall—you will easily become, if you already aren't, a part of these statistics.

Caring for your mental wellness should be a top priority. Having a plan in place for taking care of your emotional welfare at the outset will help you tremendously when you face the challenges that will surely arise.

I've compiled a list of proven strategies and real actions you can take to protect your mental health.

STRATEGIES FOR PROTECTING
YOUR MENTAL HEALTH

Strategy (What)	Real Actions (How)
Establish DEI governance structure.	• Determine early on how you are going to organize the work.
Set boundaries.	• Establish expectations upfront. Once a roadmap and KPIs are established, stay focused on the pre-determined work.
	• Clearly communicate the plan, roles, and responsibilities.
	• Evaluate situations and respond based on whether you can actually help the situation or person.
	• Assess the severity of a situation and determine a response timeline accordingly.
	• Create a system that requires people to do certain work or education on their own before you get involved. For example, create a list of resources already available on your organization's website or intranet.
Communicate your needs.	• Schedule regular (at least biweekly) check-ins with your manager to share progress, opportunities, and needs.
	• When discussing needs, be prepared to show evidence.
Delegate.	• Use the time and resources of your team, the DEI council, ERG leaders, etc., to accomplish certain tasks.

Strategy (What)	Real Actions (How)
Build your support system.	• Identify allies and sponsors. • Find a mentor and/or community of allies to support your success and professional development.

These self-care strategies and actions are *internal*—meaning they're ones you can set and implement within your organization when it comes to this work. You can also add *external* strategies for support too. These would be practices you engage outside of work, such as exercise, healthy eating, or leisure reading.

Think of your life in terms of six major areas: physical, psychological, emotional, spiritual, personal, and professional. Most of us tend to focus on one or two areas and forget the others, but take a moment to think of an activity or two you can use to support yourself and your mental health in each of the areas.

Then review the chart above and notice: Which internal strategies resonates with you most? Which one do you feel might be a challenge for you to implement and stick to? Why?

Protecting your mental health will be nonnegotiable as you seek to prevent diversity fatigue and sustain the work on this journey. You do not have to try every strategy at once. However, I encourage you to choose at least two internal strategies and two external strategies as part of your preparations. Put your mental health plan together before you start working on the DEI strategic roadmap for your organization.

Rule #2: Use your own context to determine language.

The second rule of engagement surrounds the usage of acronyms. There are so many! DEI, DEIB, DIB, EDI, DEIBA—which is it? This question is important, especially considering the backlash again DEI work. As a result, some organizations are reframing how they discuss DEI and the language they use.

For example, in a conversation with Dr. Tracie Jones-Barrett, deputy equity chief in the School of Humanities, Arts, and Social Sciences at MIT, she shared what was once called DEI is now BAC. The "B" stands for Belonging, the "A" stands for Achievement, and the "C" stands for Composition. They have adopted these terms *belonging, achievement,* and *composition* because they believe it better reflects how MIT defines community, its focus, and its values, rather than the more commonly used *diversity, equity,* and *inclusion.*

The bottom line is every organization has its own reasons and rationale for the acronyms they choose to guide this work. The Centre for Global Inclusion, a team of nearly 115 researchers and experts worldwide that created the Global Diversity, Equity, and Inclusion Benchmarks (GDEIB),[8] determined that DEI was the most appropriate and universally understood acronym. In this book, and in my work generally, the primary acronym used is DEI. Depending on where your organization is on the journey or where your greatest opportunities are for propelling the work forward, you may use another acronym altogether. That's perfectly fine. Whatever name you give it, it's ultimately about operationalizing the work in the field. For added convenience, I have made available a full listing of commonly used acronyms in the appendix.

Now that we have established our rules for engagement, let's get into why you are really here—the *how* of DEI practice.

How to Use This Book

It is one thing to know a massive amount of work lies ahead. It's quite another to know how to get it done, what to do, or where to start. Your ultimate goal is to make thz work effective. This book will help you create a roadmap for substantive and sustainable DEI change strategies to propel your organization forward. Here are some suggestions about using this book that will allow you to evolve your DEI practice most successfully.

First, we want to acknowledge that every experience you've had with others will come to this work with you. We carry our history and lived experiences within us. Your cultural background is valuable and undoubtedly impacts the way that you approach this DEI work. However, to make it all last, you must use the developed framework, create your own strategy, use cultural intelligence, and follow your roadmap.

Whether you have been engaged in this work for three months or three decades, avoid the temptation and pressure to chase quick results by skipping steps in the change process. I encourage you to stay the course of each step, even if you think you are beyond a particular phase. Following the steps in the recommended sequence will help you stay organized in this process, and help you fill any gaps or missed opportunities you may notice along the way.

Second, we all need to be realistic. I launched a course called DEI Propel in January 2022. Like this book, the course was designed to help DEI leaders and allies develop a strategic roadmap for their organization. After the inaugural cohort of leaders from across the United States completed the course, I asked for their feedback—especially on what could be improved. The responses were overwhelmingly positive, but the insight of one participant, who happened to be the manager of diversity and inclusion programs at a large global life sciences company, struck me. She said, "The course was excellent. In fact, it exceeded my expectations. The framework and process to develop a roadmap were clear. But what about the delusional organization or leader?"

The word *delusional* felt like a risky one to use, and maybe even sounds harsh. But she went on to share how she's been in the DEI space for years and has observed first-hand how many organizations can be in denial—and thus delusional—about their progress. Point-blank, many think they are farther along than they are.

Sometimes, this truth is uncomfortable to acknowledge. Realistically, failing to do an honest and searching assessment of our organization should be far more uncomfortable. Being accurate and truthful about your organization's current state, as well as its commitment and willingness to change, will be essential in this process. Your candor and humility will model the way and embolden others to be honest on their journeys. Doing DEI work well favors modesty and honoring the truth without any delusion.

If you're just getting started on your journey, that's okay. Many, perhaps most, organizations are in the same position. What's not okay or helpful is the temptation to pretend we've made more progress than we have or confusing hit-and-miss DEI activities and performative outputs with successful outcomes.

Finally, be open and courageous. Consider different per-spectives. Commit to unlearning erroneous beliefs. Be open to learning new approaches and trying fresh efforts, even if pre-vious attempts have failed. Enjoy the process. Keep an open mind about the growth opportunities that will emerge. Your openness will create space for the work to take hold.

As you may be able to tell by now, this book is interactive.

There may be times when you will need to pause and reflect. Truthfulness and sincerity will help you accomplish the tasks with greater ease. The moments of reflection built into this book will also build on previously covered areas—which is another great reason not to skip steps.

Here's a suggestion: Take a minute right now to pause and reflect. How are you feeling? Which ideas that you've read so far stand out or stick with you?

You Are Here

When you're looking at a map or shopping mall directory, you'll find stickers marked "You are here." These markings help you see where you are in relation to your desired destination. Likewise, as you begin the journey to make DEI work last in your organization, it's necessary to identify your starting point. While we may be clear on where we want to go, knowing our starting point is necessary to create a clear and complete roadmap.

You've created your mental health strategy and reviewed the rules of engagement. You've also taken time to check in on your current feelings about this work. Now you're ready to begin the deeper work of assessing the state of your organization when it comes to DEI.

You can ask specific questions to get a clear picture of where your organization needs to focus its efforts. To start, take a look at the DEI Maturity Model below. This model provides you with a way to think about this and to benchmark the progress of your organization's DEI efforts.

The example indicates five stages of progress. Read about each stage carefully. At what phase of maturity would you say your organization is now? (Be sure to answer with honesty!)

DEI MATURITY MODEL

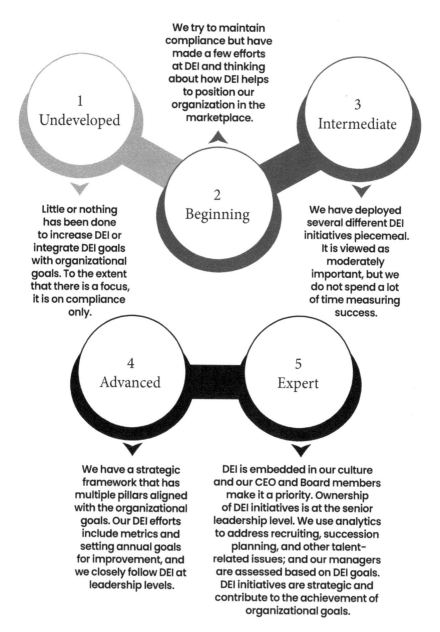

We try to maintain compliance but have made a few efforts at DEI and thinking about how DEI helps to position our organization in the marketplace.

1 Undeveloped

3 Intermediate

2 Beginning

Little or nothing has been done to increase DEI or integrate DEI goals with organizational goals. To the extent that there is a focus, it is on compliance only.

We have deployed several different DEI initiatives piecemeal. It is viewed as moderately important, but we do not spend a lot of time measuring success.

4 Advanced

5 Expert

We have a strategic framework that has multiple pillars aligned with the organizational goals. Our DEI efforts include metrics and setting annual goals for improvement, and we closely follow DEI at leadership levels.

DEI is embedded in our culture and our CEO and Board members make it a priority. Ownership of DEI initiatives is at the senior leadership level. We use analytics to address recruiting, succession planning, and other talent-related issues; and our managers are assessed based on DEI goals. DEI initiatives are strategic and contribute to the achievement of organizational goals.

Other questions that may help you assess your organization's current state include:

- What are the biggest challenges your organization faces regarding DEI?
- Who has been instrumental in driving DEI work?
- Which DEI efforts have been implemented?
- Which DEI efforts worked? How did you measure success?
- Which DEI efforts failed? Why?

DEI work is not easy, but the fact that you're reading this book says you're open to the journey. I'm excited about partnering with you to propel this work forward within your organization. Progress is possible, but lasting change takes time. Because DEI work is all about change, the journey to operationalizing the work will also take time. Allow yourself permission to slow down, and do the work the right way.

DEI Propel™ Framework

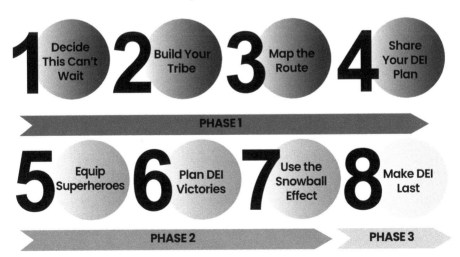

I designed the DEI Propel Framework using evidence-based change management strategies. This framework has three phases with eight chronological steps. As you consider the eight steps, think deeply about which step you believe your organization or department is in.

The three phases of this framework mimic social psychologist Kurt Lewin's Change Theory.[9] The steps in each phase build upon each other. This means that even if you feel like you've already completed a step in the process, instead of immediately checking the box, walk through each step with care, attention, and time. And remember, we don't want to be delusional or well-intentioned. We want to be effective.

Let's take a closer look at the three phases.

Phase 1: Unfreezing the Current State

Here's a common scenario I encounter with potential clients:

> Potential Client: Can you come and facilitate unconscious bias training with our employees?
>
> Me: Okay, let's discuss it. How do you know your employees need unconscious bias training, and how does this fit within your broader DEI strategy?
>
> Potential Client: Well, we think it's an important topic. We don't have a strategy yet, but we want to get some training started.

Now, is unconscious bias a real issue? Absolutely! However, facilitating any training without a clear understanding of your current state often doesn't produce the expected result or impact. As a first step, and as we'll discuss in detail later in the book, you need to conduct an assessment. What does the data tell you about the state of diversity, equity, and inclusion in your organization? How do your employees—especially those who are underrepresented—perceive the organization's commitment to this? What systems, processes, or practices in the organization are barriers to DEI work?

After completing your analysis, you'll create a DEI vision and strategic roadmap to help unfreeze the current state or status quo. You'll use the data to obtain buy-in and demonstrate to others across the organization why the work is necessary and urgent. How well and consistently we communicate with employees during this stage of the work is a critical predictor of the outcome we want.

PHASE 1: UNFREEZING THE CURRENT STATE

Step 1: Decide This Can't Wait	**Help** your organization understand the importance and urgency of DEI to obtain buy-in.
Step 2: Build Your Tribe	**Organize** a team of DEI leaders and allies to lead the work.
Step 3: Map the Route	**Develop** a DEI vision and data-driven strategic roadmap.
Step 4: Share the DEI Plan	**Communicate** the DEI vision and strategy constantly and consistently.

Phase 2: Introducing New DEI Practices

Even the best-developed strategy means nothing if it's not put into action. Phase 2 requires successful implementation of the strategy and new practices.

This work should be shared by everyone, not just the CDO or DEI committee. But before you assign others to join in the work, you must empower them with skills, resources, and confidence. This includes your passionate DEI allies. Passion is good, but it doesn't necessarily translate to competence in this space.

It's also important to keep people motivated by creating and celebrating short-term DEI wins. For example, in the first year of your strategy rollout, you might create employee resource groups (ERGs) or develop an executive sponsorship program for historically excluded groups in your organization. This could enable you to diversify top leadership. When this happens, celebrate and broadly communicate these wins.

PHASE 2: INTRODUCING NEW DEI PRACTICES

Step 5: Equip Superheroes	**Educate and upskill** DEI allies, managers, and others so the work is shared.
Step 6: Plan DEI Victories	**Plan and celebrate** progress and wins, big and small.
Step 7: Use the Snowball Effect	**Use** progress and successes to create more success and organizational change.

Phase 3: Making It Last

Two of the most important questions we should consider as we go about this work are:

1. How will we measure impact?

2. How will we sustain our efforts?

There are multiple ways to measure impact. These can include key performance indicators (KPIs), such as increasing the number of historically excluded people in influential leadership roles or developing a supplier diversity program. The key thing to remember is that every strategy should have a metric and some accountability tied to it.

Sustaining this work requires ongoing and consistent leadership engagement and regular assessment, communication, and celebration of progress. Show people the "before versus after" impact. Build in accountability and, when necessary, make adjustments to your strategic roadmap.

PHASE 3: MAKE THE DEI CHANGES LAST

Step 8: Make DEI Last	**Demonstrate** the relationship between changing behaviors and systems, leadership commitment, and a more inclusive and equitable organizational culture.

Creating a culture where diversity, equity, and inclusion is part of the DNA of an organization takes time, but it's possible—and it's the only way to authentically and effectively create an inclusive organization where everyone thrives. Now that you have a framework, you are ready to get down to business. It is time to learn the *how* of DEI so you can make it last in your organization.

PHASE 1
UNFREEZING THE CURRENT STATE

Step 1

DECIDE THIS CAN'T WAIT

S OME TIME AGO, a client asked me, "Do you know about the Class of 2020?" I didn't. She told me it referred to the massive cohort of CDOs hired by organizations across the country and the globe shortly after the murder of George Floyd. She was a member of this group. She was, in fact, the first-ever chief diversity officer hired at Saks Fifth Avenue.

Before 2020, there had been a surge in DEI initiatives across American industries and organizations. In fact, between 2015 and 2020, diversity roles in the United States alone increased by 71 percent.[1] But 2020 was the year many organizations elevated diversity and inclusion to the top of the agenda. In a review of new hires conducted by Russell Reynolds Associates, researchers found that the hiring of new diversity chiefs has nearly tripled since 2020.[2] In some cases, as many as a dozen new positions were being filled monthly. The 2021 study demonstrated that more than sixty firms appointed their first-ever diversity chief since May 2020.

On the other hand, progress has been limited or stalled. Those leading the work often express frustrations about this with me, and the sense of urgency in many organizations seems to be waning. The Reynolds research sums it up this way:

> Good intentions drove much of the rise in CDO appointment since 2020. However, these appointments often

failed to come with business support, resource investment, and concern for the personal demands placed on CDOs.[3]

The first step in developing an effective DEI strategic roadmap is recognizing the urgency of the work. I'm not talking about creating diversity positions for optics or rushing to performative acts. What's needed is a burning conviction that DEI matters, and it matters now. Such urgency is critical for creating lasting organizational transformation. This transformation requires a shift in mindset to a "this can't wait" attitude. This includes helping everyone across the organization understand that the need for DEI is now, not later. It also includes helping them understand their buy-in is critical to creating change. In all truth, this work can't wait.

As you go through the process of developing your DEI strategy, you'll be tempted to skip steps, especially the first four steps in this first phase. Do not skip these steps. Do not succumb to the pressure to immediately produce something. This is especially important when you know your organization's current efforts are at least partially performative, resulting in more output-driven, rather than outcome-driven, actions. Recognizing and leaning into this sense of urgency is the first step in developing your DEI strategic roadmap. We need to stay here as long as necessary, and only then can we work through each subsequent step.

Moving forward in the *how* of this work requires you to understand the challenges that can impact your organization's ability to create a sense of urgency surrounding DEI efforts. One of the challenges can be complacency. Kotter reminds us that high complacency coupled with low urgency leads to limited effort. If a large percentage of your employees are content, then leadership has not done a good job helping them understand why this work is important and why it's important now. Starting from this position will only yield a failed DEI effort. We cannot move the work forward if too many people are complacent about the work, and we've not done a good job creating a sense of urgency if complacency rules the day.

During one of my DEI Propel courses, a DEI manager at a large global company asked, "How do you create urgency when the organization is performing well financially with very little emphasis on DEI?" This wasn't the first time I'd heard this question. If bottom-line results for an organization are strong, it's quite easy to dismiss the need for and value of DEI. Of course, one thing to consider is the missed potential for even greater and sustained profits. If you have a diverse and culturally intelligent team of employees at all levels of the organization and you have created an inclusive and equitable work environment, the research is clear: performance improves, and the bottom line is positively impacted.[4] While the organization may be doing well financially, why not go from good to great?

Another challenge is resistance by those who don't believe in or understand the need for DEI. Every organization has such individuals, and sometimes they're in leadership and other influential positions. For different reasons, one of which often includes fear, they are averse to the strategies and efforts needed to move the DEI work forward. It can be tempting to say, "Ignore them and move on." But it's important not to underestimate the magnitude and impact of their resistance—and the resistance they communicate to others. DEI resistors can have power and influence, and you are going to have some resistance. I always advise not giving the resistors all your energy. Preserve your mental health. Don't spend all your energy trying to convince people against the work, but do understand the resistance.

We can sometimes do things to win support from resistors. Change is possible. But if, after sincere and persistent efforts, you find they still don't support your DEI goals and strategies, move on. And by moving on, I don't mean you should simply say, "Okay, well, they're going to resist," and then ignore them. You want to maintain an awareness of your resistors. Later, you'll learn how to address resistors within your teams.

A third and final key to establishing a sense of urgency is getting buy-in. When I ask the "What's keeping you up at night?" question in live sessions, I often hear "Getting buy-in." Getting buy-in keeps DEI leaders and allies up at night because it requires closing the gap between logic and emotion.

Part of getting buy-in is understanding that you've got to give people a combination of head and heart information. I encourage most organizations I work with to start with the head. The head information would be all of those data points we know are important. The examples are ones we hear often:

- There's no diversity on the leadership team.

- Women and people of color aren't compensated at the same rate as their white counterparts in comparable positions.

- Our policies don't address the needs of employees who are part of the neurodiverse and differently-abled communities.

- Attrition rates for millennials are high.

- Patients of color express dissatisfaction with how they're being served compared to majority patients.

This kind of data is incredibly valuable in terms of helping people see why these disparities continue to stall efforts to create a diverse, inclusive, and equitable organization. What does your data say? For example, when the data reveals a disconnect between your goal to have more diverse representation across the organization and the lack of a diverse talent pool, use this information to determine where to strategically focus your efforts. Start where there is glaring evidence of inequity. Then work hard to identify the not-so-obvious ones and integrate actions into your strategy to address them.

Then there's the second area of focus: appealing to the heart. This involves creating space for the sharing of real stories and lived experiences, especially from individuals and cultural groups who are underrepresented or who have been historically excluded.

In my trainings, for example, I sometimes share the story of what happened at an event hosted by my former boss when my husband and I sat down at a table with an older white woman. She asked how I knew my boss who happened to be white. When I told her we worked together, she said, "Oh...so, are you his scheduler?"

My husband and I looked at each other, not completely surprised but also disappointed and admittedly a bit angered. I responded, "No, I'm actually one of the vice presidents, but what made you assume I was his scheduler?"

I don't recall her counter-response, but I remember thinking how devaluing her comment was. That is what a microaggression looks like. It was informed by bias and assumptions about the kind of role someone who looks like me would fill.

There is absolutely nothing wrong with being a scheduler. In fact, in some contexts, especially in other parts of the world, it is deemed a high-level role. But not in this context. Instead, it implied low rank and low significance. It was an insulting inquiry into my credibility to sit at the table. A more appropriate and respectful question from the woman would have been, "What do you do at the organization?" That question brings no assumptions with it. I could be the scheduler or the president of the company.

When I share this story, others begin to see these types of microaggressions are real and happen often. They are also a reminder that your role, rank, or position in the organization doesn't protect or exempt you from them. Moreover, microaggressions can undermine DEI work. Imagine if that woman was in charge of talent acquisition at her organization, or if she were a department head? How might her biases impact her hiring and promotion of people who look like me?

Data alone doesn't inspire us to change our behaviors; ordinary people and stories do. Research tells us that storytelling is a very powerful strategy. Appealing to the heart through stories invites perspective taking. This is the idea of standing in someone else's shoes and understanding life's experiences from their point of view. One study found that taking the perspective of others "may have a lasting positive effect on diversity-related outcomes by increasing individuals' internal motivation to respond without prejudice."[5] Real stories build emotional value when appealing to people's hearts. Think about what stories and lived experiences from those within your organization might bring the data of the organization to life. Why might this matter to the people within your organization?

As you make the case or establish a sense of urgency, yes, you want to identify pain points from a data perspective. However, you also want to get to the heart of the matter by sharing real stories and real experiences of individuals who felt they did not receive equitable care. You want to hear from the team member who is consistently on the receiving end of microaggressions.

As a DEI change leader, you need a hybrid of data, insights, and information to help others understand this work can't wait. By appealing to both the head and the heart, your efforts demonstrate the vital importance of DEI and will have a greater likelihood of connecting with employees at every level of the organization.

How Much Buy-In Is Necessary to Effect Change?

How much employee buy-in do you need? The most successful DEI efforts happen when the majority of employees share responsibility for the work and have the competence and confidence to support the commitment. But what does that look like in practice?

Let's review some of the change management benchmarks that Kotter and other experts highlight. When talking about top leadership—and I'm pointing to the very top echelon of the organization here—there should be 100 percent buy-in. Senior leadership sets the stage and should model the way for DEI work. If you have leaders at this level who are not convinced DEI should be a priority and are not willing to help lead the work, that is a serious problem. It will almost always undermine the work. This is where the CEO or president needs to step in and make clear that engagement and help leading this work are not optional for top leaders in the organization. Top leaders in the organization are responsible for helping others understand that DEI can't wait.

As a rule, at least 75 percent of middle management staff

must also be engaged. Additionally, the majority of non-management employees or individual contributors should understand why this is urgent. They should be committed, equipped to support the work, and eager to get others equally engaged.

Some might argue, "But what about the sticky middle? What about that 25 percent of managers or other employees who may not be committed or engaged, or just flat-out resist?" Two notes on this—first, ideally your goal should be to have every leader and employee across the organization committed to this work, and every effort should be made to secure their buy-in and engagement. (I talk more about how to do this in Step 7.) But second, the reality is that everyone may not understand the work and there may be resistors. Evidence-based change management practices tell us that with full support from the top levels and with majority support (75 percent) at every other level of the organization, we can effectively move DEI work forward and achieve organizational change.

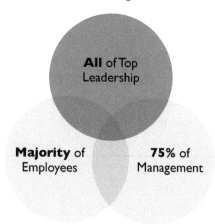

I consulted with a large healthcare system that did a great job using this approach. They had hard data and lots of it. Their DEI data collection and analysis process exposed a wide range of inequities in patient care, particularly in the area of racial equity. The top leadership roles had limited diversity, and they discovered bias in their recruitment and hiring practices. The data was clear: a DEI strategy was needed.

However, the leadership understood data alone wasn't enough to get more than thirty thousand very busy clinical and nonclinical staff to understand the urgency of diversity, equity, and inclusion and to support moving it forward. Their comprehensive DEI strategy included a number of strategic actions intended to get at people's hearts. These ranged from facilitating numerous learning and development opportunities to hosting a "Day of Understanding." This event was intentionally held on Juneteenth, the federal holiday that commemorates the emancipation of enslaved African Americans, and its purpose was to create space for authentic and courageous conversations about the experiences and history of African American staff across the healthcare system and broader community. There was an opportunity for storytelling, perspective taking, and asking questions.

Additionally, I developed and facilitated numerous sessions with hundreds of staff on topics such as cultural intelligence and unconscious bias. These interactive learning experiences were filled with underrepresented staff who shared their stories, experiences, and perspectives. Overall, employee feedback from these combined experiences was very positive.

This work of the heart significantly enhanced the level of employee engagement in the organization's DEI work and won over some of the employees who were in the sticky middle. If your organization has made a strong case using a hybrid of head and heart, and the majority of employees respond positively and engage well, you can feel confident you're moving in a good direction.

Leverage Leadership

Everything in our approach to how to do DEI work is driven by the desire to propel organizations and teams forward. This means that some sort of action is required to impart or initiate motion. I previously mentioned the need for leadership buy-in as the foundation of DEI efforts. When it comes to the "now, not later" approach, it's best to propel DEI work forward—not only by gaining leadership buy-in but also by leveraging their authority and influence.

Start by having frank conversations with leaders. Confide in them that where leaders aren't clear about their commitment to and expectations around DEI, the chances of DEI work propelling forward are slim to none. The same holds true for modeling inclusive leadership behaviors.

Here's an example to show you what I mean. I was in a discussion about strategy with a team of executives at a mid-sized manufacturing company in the Midwest when the CEO shared about an anonymous note he had received from an employee. The employee expressed concern the organization had fallen prey to socially progressive "woke" rhetoric, and threatened to leave the organization if things continued in that direction. After describing the message, the CEO said, "I wish I knew who the employee was—so I could tell them goodbye."

This is the level of commitment top leaders in an organization need to demonstrate if they are serious about this work. Did the CEO want to lose colleagues? Did he not care about this one employee? Certainly not! As our discussion deepened, he went on to say he wished he could sit with the note writer, and have an honest and psychologically safe conversation. He wanted to understand why the employee felt the way he or she did. He also hoped for an opportunity to help them see how important this work is, and to bring them on board with the effort. We all realized the CEO's initial comment was symbolic. He was clear that the leadership was not going to shrink back on their firm commitment to this work.

Next, discuss why DEI efforts are critical to your organization's success. Remember to cite the proven data (appeal to their head), and utilize impactful stories (appeal to their heart) in your approach.

Once you have made the case for DEI change with leadership, get a firm commitment. Their obligation is more than a verbal agreement or their endorsement of you doing the work. The obligation requires action on their part. They need to understand they must play a key role in the work—but don't be surprised if they are uncomfortable and unsure of what they should do. They are not DEI experts.

Be prepared to do some educating and upskilling with your top leadership. You may have to help them develop action items and provide them with additional support, resources, and encouragement, and that's okay. We'll discuss this more in Step 5. For now, the goal of the change process is to help the leaders and managers in your organization see and communicate a sense of urgency around DEI. Knowing they will help lead the work will add confidence and credibility to your approach as you prepare to roll out your DEI strategy across the rest of the organization. It will also help you maintain the boundaries you set around your mental health.

At this point, you may think this seems quite a bit easier said than done. I'm not going to sugar coat it: yes, this is hard work. There's no way around it. But it's only hard, not impossible. The work is easier if you understand that part of your role as a DEI leader or ally is equipping leaders and helping them see themselves as change leaders. Then, as part of your strategy, you can leverage them to get the work done. By leveraging leadership, you have a significantly greater chance at increasing buy-in and engagement across the organization and distributing the load of the work.

Propelling Actions

If creating a sense of urgency and getting buy-in is where you feel stuck or frustrated, there are proven change management strategies (what) to help you move through this first step. There are also specific, real actions (how) connected to making those DEI strategies operational. I recommend taking time to massage them and think about which efforts will work best for your organization or team.

Create a DEI Crisis.

The first strategy is creating a DEI crisis. Now, when I say that, I don't mean pull a fire alarm or sound off sirens and send everyone into panic mode. This is not about conveying something awful. But it is about communicating this is serious work, and it's important to address right now. There are so many reasons we need to do this work, and most of them involve a genuine sense of urgency. If we don't secure the needed sense of urgency in this step, that will lead to many missed opportunities, and your organization will get left behind. Most significantly, the employees we claim to value so deeply will suffer.

The most obvious and well-known example of a genuine and tragic DEI crisis is the murder of George Floyd in 2020. Out of this somber, heartbreaking event came a major national and global reckoning. Following Floyd's murder, hundreds of organizations made unprecedented pledges and committed billions of dollars to confront racism and address diversity, equity, and inclusion within their organizations. It was a clear crisis and people responded.

Unfortunately, and despite the efforts spawned in the wake of this national tragedy, progress in DEI has remained very slow. One reason for this sluggish pace of change, I believe, is that organizations didn't follow a process like the one outlined in this book. They reacted to a crisis but did not commit to the deep work involved at every level of the organization to create substantive and sustainable change. They failed to heed the counsel we've all heard: "Never waste a crisis."

Another example of a less publicized DEI crisis could be that you are losing employees of color at an alarming rate. Or perhaps your competitors are much farther along in their DEI efforts than you are. Some surveys show that Gen Z, which is the future of the workforce, seeks employers committed to DEI. In fact, an iCIMS study reveals that 58 percent of Gen Z applicants expect to learn about a company's DEI efforts during the interview process.[6] A more recent Bloomberg article highlighted that almost three-quarters of this younger generation want their employer to focus on diversity initiatives.[7] If you are not attracting or retaining the best of this generation in your workforce, that in itself may be a DEI crisis.

You could even look no further than your own employee workforce, and create opportunities for underrepresented groups in your organization to tell their personal stories and experiences (based on their comfort level) as a way to raise overall employee awareness of these issues and their real-world urgency.

When you thoughtfully look around, you will find no shortage of crises. You need to identify and clearly communicate the ones that apply to your organization so they catch people's attention, and make them realize the need to do something different.

Share current data with employees.

A second strategy for helping your organization see the need for this work is now and urgent is by sharing current, quality data with employees. This is especially important for executive-level leaders in the organization.

To be clear, appealing to both the heart and head of leadership is important because it protects DEI work from becoming performative. But in addition to the deep belief that it is the moral thing to do, and in addition to learning about the lived experiences of today's employees, top leadership needs to see the business value of DEI. This is critical because leaders are required to ensure the bottom-line success of the organization. If they don't understand the added value of DEI, they are less likely to give and approve the time and resources needed to move the work forward.

All employees in the organization should see compelling data as well. Employees should understand how diversity, equity, and inclusion impact their departments and teams. And the data should be disaggregated, by which I mean breaking it down to show data specific to cultural groups. For example, what do African Americans on the team feel? What about the different generations or those who self-identify as nonbinary? This process often tells a fresh and different part of the story, particularly for underrepresented groups across the organization.

To emphasize this point, I'm reminded of the research and work on *targeted universalism*. This term, coined by john a.

powell, director of the Othering and Belonging Institute and Professor of law and African American studies at University of California, Berkeley, emphasizes the need for a balanced and two-pronged approach to DEI. The broad DEI goal is that everyone is positively impacted by its efforts. At the same time, organizations need to take a targeted approach to meet the unique needs of specific populations within the organization.[8]

Here's why targeted universalism and the use of disaggregated data are important. Once, I was helping a client develop a DEI strategy and asked, "Do you have any solid data to support the development of a data-driven strategic plan?" She said, proudly, "Yes! Every year, we do a company-wide survey to get feedback on how employees feel about working here and our culture. We consistently receive high marks across the board, including the specific questions we ask about DEI. In fact, our company has won awards for our efforts for three consecutive years."

Impressed, I asked if they could share the data with me. As I began to disaggregate the data based on different demographic and cultural groups (women, people of color, LGBTQIA+, etc.), I saw a different picture than the one that had been so confidently painted for me. The underrepresented populations didn't view the organization the same way the dominant group of white employees did. They voiced concerns about perceived inequities, lack of promotional opportunities, lack of diversity at the top of the organization, and more. When we looked deeper at the hard data, several of these perceptions proved to be realities.

As you prepare to share data in your organization, be sure to do a thorough and fair analysis of the facts and numbers so employees have a full picture of the organization's current state and why there should be an urgency to change. Once you've tackled the real data, there are several things you can do. Using data from DEI assessments, employee pulse or engagement surveys, or inclusion questionnaires, you can share a combination of qualitative (narratives and personal stories) and quantitative data. Additionally, share diversity representation data across the employee life cycle—talent acquisition (attracting and hiring), promotion and development, and retention—and at all levels of the organization.

Listen.

Yes, it sounds simple and basic, but we know listening is a skill. It requires perspective-taking, which is the ability to step outside our own experiences to imagine the emotions, perceptions, and motivations of another individual. Adam Galinsky, a scholar and vice dean for DEI at Columbia University, has completed research proving that perspective-taking increases the likelihood that individuals will not only be less discriminatory in their thoughts and behaviors but will actually develop more positive viewpoints.[9] It's not always easy, especially when it's information we don't want to hear. It's much easier and less painful to become defensive.

Galinsky's research also shows that holding personal power actually reduces the ability to understand how others see, think, and feel. I see this often when I'm facilitating DEI needs assessments with organizations. Leaders want feedback, but they don't want feedback.

In this first step of preparing to develop a DEI roadmap, it's critical to listen to how employees feel about your organization's DEI commitment and strategies. This means listening without making judgments or taking a position. Not only do listening and perspective-taking require skill; they also require humility and follow-up. Once we hear reliable feedback, we can't unhear it. And there's this: the fastest way to lose credibility and momentum is to hear the responses and do nothing about them.

I love how the financial technology company Affirm developed a listening strategy for DEI.[10] To understand the impact of their work, they measure DEI feedback and sentiments from employees (called Affirmers) and track progress over time. Like many organizations, they conduct a bi-annual engagement survey. They also facilitate just-in-time surveys to understand specific pain points related to DEI. Affirm also launched Suggestion Ox, an online feedback platform that allows for anonymous and two-way feedback from Affirmers on various DEI topics at the organization. Given that one of their core values is People Come First, you might expect these kind of efforts. The actions and behaviors of organizations and leaders don't always align with their words, but at Affirm, they do. No wonder the outcomes are so positive.

Affirm's efforts to listen are commendable. More importantly, because the company has acted on the feedback, they have seen a significant increase in positive sentiments regarding how employees from diverse backgrounds perceive DEI at Affirm. In addition, the level of engagement has increased.

Actively and authentically listening to your employees is a powerful and proven strategy to help create a sense of urgency. One way you could do this is by encouraging leadership time with underrepresented groups. This can be done through focus groups, Days of Understanding, listening campaigns, inclusion dialogues, and the like. You can also practice reciprocal mentoring. You might also create employee experience touchpoints, such as surveys, team meetings, focus groups, or one-on-one meetings with supervisors.

Be honest and transparent about your DEI realities and challenges.

More and more organizations are publishing annual DEI transparency reports. It began mostly in the corporate space and has extended to academic and government sectors. Even the United States Office of Personnel Government published, for the first time in history, their DEIA Annual Report in 2022.[11] But why?

I believe there are a few driving reasons. First, organizations are attempting to demonstrate the importance of building in accountability, both with their employees and with the broader community. In fact, research has shown that when pressured to improve their DEI efforts, organizations are more likely to make changes when the public is inclined to notice them and to avoid changes when they are not being watched and held accountable.[12] Second, they want to publicly highlight their DEI efforts, progress, and successes. Organizations want to share their DEI journey and real stories of change and impact at both the individual and systems level. They do this by appealing to the reader's head (data) and heart (stories).

Producing and publishing these reports also reveals challenges, weaknesses, and opportunities to improve. While these revelations may make your organization vulnerable to attacks and criticism, I believe the consequences of not being transparent outweigh the risk and fear of being attacked. This is especially true given the current social landscape and conversations around corporate social responsibility and environmental, social, and governance reporting.

As I've worked with organizations on their DEI journeys, I've seen employees and other stakeholders become more quick to extend grace and support to leaders of organizations who are making genuine efforts to improve. Just as important, they communicate on a regular and consistent basis. Transparency has become the norm and can be a powerful part of your strategy to create a sense of urgency. I recommend producing an annual DEI transparency report. You might also facilitate quarterly town hall meetings that allow others to voice their experience and feedback.

Bombard employees with data on future rewards and benefits of DEI work.

I mentioned earlier how important it is to help leadership understand the added value of DEI. This is true for all employees. If people don't see and understand how these changes will benefit them as individuals and the organization as a whole, your efforts will stall—and they need to understand this early on.

Whenever I'm facilitating any type of DEI learning and development experience with a client, I always start and end the session with an "Imagine if..." talk. *Imagine if* we get this DEI thing right, how much better we'll work together; how much more creative, innovative, and competitive we will be; how much better we'll serve our customers, clients, or community. *Just imagine.* Yes, there is a true business case to be made for DEI—and you would do well to develop one for your organization.

Additionally, the research is clear: organizations with greater diversity that effectively leverage that diversity by developing culturally intelligent leaders and staff outperform other organizations in countless ways.[13]

As you can see, operationalizing this work doesn't have to be mysterious. You have probably heard of many of these strategies during your work in this space. The way forward is found by choosing the real actions that can be utilized and sustained within your organization. At each step of creating your strategic roadmap, you will have the opportunity to choose which strategies and actions work best for your organization, and then customize them to fit your DEI journey. These are the same actions I use when working with organizations across the globe. There is no one-size-fits-all solution, but each approach can be contextualized for propulsion.

CALLING IN VERSUS CALLING OUT

Years ago, I facilitated an unconscious bias certification program with a team of staff and faculty at an Ivy League university. At one point in the program, we discussed the importance of understanding, respecting, and navigating cultural differences. One of the participants, a Caucasian woman, shared how in a prior life she was a cosmetologist. She recalled having a conversation with a group of African American women where she shared her vision to serve women from all backgrounds, including women of color. During the conversation, she touched the hair of one of the women. Most Black women, including myself, feel pretty strongly that this is a serious violation of our culture and space. Not only did the woman whose hair had been touched become upset, but the entire group was also offended and instantly shut the conversation down. The woman confided in our group that, still all these years later, she felt bad about the incident yet was unsure what she did wrong.

As a response to this woman's story, several of the Black women in our session gracefully called her in. They took time to explain why her actions were inappropriate and offensive. At the same time, they challenged her. One woman commented, "Even if those women chose not to explain what you did wrong, why didn't you take the time to educate yourself?" Another asked, "And did you apologize? Educating yourself would have created an opportunity for you, as a Caucasian woman, to be an ally and help educate others."

Their response was a calling in, rather than a calling out, and this is the preferred approach. When we call people in, we invite them into the conversation and work. We don't attack or shame them—that's calling out. Calling in makes room for challenging each other, having courageous conversations, and holding people accountable. We honor the truth by acknowledging our past and present realities when it comes to DEI. In fact, these are all important elements for creating the kind of change necessary for substantive progress. What's more, they require us to become comfortable with being uncomfortable. That requires courage and skill on the part of everyone.

In her book *We Can't Talk about That at Work*, Mary-Frances Winters reminds us that the most persuasive reason for building the skills necessary to talk about polarizing topics at work is that they are already being talked about or thought about, and more than you may think. These productive conversations leave people feeling whole, and they ultimately result in better teamwork, productivity, and engagement.

A while back, I was listening to a powerful dialogue about comfort zones between Robin DiAngelo, author of *White Fragility*, and Resmaa Menakem, a trauma specialist and author of *My Grandmother's Hands*. Both argued that the forces of comfort are seductive. People are easily lured in the direction of staying in a comfortable space because it allows them to ignore and dismiss the harsh realities of racism and racist systems. But yielding to this comes at a cost. White people want to move on to the next thing, but people of color don't have the option of doing so. As a consequence, power and control remain in the hands of the dominant culture.

With all of this said, shaming people still isn't helpful. We want to challenge people to acknowledge hard facts, and understand that everyone is a critical part of the needed change. Real change only happens when we are willing to become uncomfortable. In her book *The Wake Up*, Michelle MiJung Kim asks the question "How does your organization prioritize the comfort of the privileged over the safety of the marginalized?"[14] This represents the kind of questions that hold us accountable for doing the deep work of DEI.

But how we ask such questions is almost as important as the question itself. One of the best approaches is to create a psychologically safe environment where people know up front that their thinking and behavior are going to be challenged while assuring them it will be done in a way that's respectful and assumes positive intent. These conversations can happen one-on-one, in groups, during team meetings, or in a more formalized learning and development experience like the one I just described. Whatever the context, there should be predetermined engagement rules and a commitment on everyone's part to listen and suspend judgment.

Loretta J. Ross, a social justice leader and mentee of civil rights leader C. T. Vivian, does a fantastic job explaining the notion of calling in versus calling out in her Ted Talk.[15] She shows how calling in invites people to have an inclusive conversation, and helps folks understand why this work is important. We also share in the benefits we all receive as a result of doing this work. Calling in helps shrink the sticky middle (the 25 percent) while engaging the front lines of management.

Remember the "Are you his scheduler?" story I shared with you? Although I was not pleased with the woman's question, I intentionally used that moment to call the woman in, not out. I still held her accountable for her words but gave her the opportunity to reflect, respond, and (we hope) do better going forward. Your work on this journey may require you to do the same. I encourage you to choose the grace of calling in and the commitment of accountability.

REFLECT AND ACT

I can't stress enough how much I want this book to help you operationalize this work by focusing on how we work. I sincerely hope you'll take the examples and suggestions offered to you and figure out the best ways to integrate them within your own teams and organization. This has been one of the largest missing pieces in creating effective DEI roadmaps.

With this in mind, I hope you'll take a moment for intentional awareness and assessment at the end of each step through the "Reflect and Act" sections. I also want to offer you space, permission, and guidance for taking action—and our action starts with this first step: create a sense of "now, not later" urgency. Decide today this work can't wait any longer.

Thinking through the need for this work to be now and not later, spend time answering the following questions and prompts. Do this before moving on to the next step.

1. **Reflect.** How will you create a sense of urgency for DEI work within your organization or within your team?

2. **Act.** Choose one or two strategies from the propelling actions outlined in this step, and use these to create and communicate the urgency of need.

KEY TAKEAWAYS

• To ensure the greatest chance for moving DEI work forward, you need buy-in.

• We don't need 100 percent support. It's certainly ideal and should be the goal, but it may not be reality at the start.

• We should, however, expect 100 percent support from the top.

• If we have at least two-thirds of our managers on board, plus the majority of non-management staff, we're heading in a good direction.

• We mustn't ignore the 25 percent (the "sticky middle"), but we mustn't delay our DEI efforts because of them.

• Our preferred approach is calling in versus calling out, with accountability.

Step 2

BUILD YOUR TRIBE

THE WORK OF DEI should penetrate every level and area of your organization, yet many organizations place full responsibility in the hands of one person. They hire a single chief diversity officer, and give them all the responsibilities. They tack the responsibilities onto the job description of an HR generalist, hoping they'll do it all alone. In other cases, they hand the reins to the most enthusiastic individual in the company, usually someone from an underrepresented group in the organization and usually failing to provide that person with any staffing support or compensation.

According to a *Harvard Business Review* Study, only 12 percent of DEI leaders have a dedicated DEI team working under them.[1] That leaves a whopping 88 percent who are trying to piece it together alone. Perhaps you can relate to this. But because DEI is such a massive and long-term undertaking, it requires more than just one person to make it operational. No matter how big or small our organizations may be, this cannot be done alone. We need a tribe—and I strategically chose the word *tribe* because this work is about bringing together a diverse community of people who are committed to a similar vision.

Two things are crucial when building your tribe. First, you'll need a credible and influential team of leaders and allies to move the work forward. Second, they—the allies, in particular—need more than a passion for the work. They must be trained to understand DEI, and they must be equipped with skills and resources to be effective change leaders. (We'll talk more about how to equip them in Step 5.)

One of the fastest ways to burn out is to attempt to do this work alone. Even if you are the primary person responsible for the DEI strategy of your organization, you still need help making the work operational. Remember that movie built on the idea "Build it, and they will come"? It's an entertaining movie, but the idea is a myth. You have to build something like this together, nurture it together, and grow it together. In other words, you need to invite others to be a part of the entire process, and hope to move forward once they've accepted your invitation.

This is where Step 2—building your tribe—comes into play. It builds off the previous step of deciding this work cannot wait. Not only will building a tribe help your mental health, but it will also position you and your organization to move the work forward in a sustainable way.

It's common in organizations to find people who are excited about the work, and that's a good thing. However, as we've already noted, we need champions who have more than passion for the work. They need to be trained to understand change, how to plan change, and how to make change.

Ultimately, DEI allies should understand how to contextualize and operationalize the framework within their own departments and teams. For example, the marketing department should have a DEI strategy and understand how to integrate DEI into its marketing practices and operations. This means making it about more than the optics of diverse marketing materials. It's about recruiting, hiring, retaining, and promoting diverse talent. It's using diverse suppliers or marketing products for people who are differently abled. It's also tying key performance indicators (KPIs) to the marketing department's DEI strategy. The same would be true for every department.

Propelling Actions

Momentum is driven by action. Something must happen to initiate forward motion. When building your tribe, specific actions will start the forward motion and propel your DEI work toward success.

Identify allies quickly.

First, you want to identify your allies, and you want to do this quickly. Who are those key influential people in the organization that you know are passionate about this work? The likelihood they will have the necessary skills is pretty low, so part of your job will be equipping them with the skill they need to support the work. Again, we'll discuss this more in Step 5, but it can include taking them through a DEI course (such as DEI Propel) or compiling suggested readings and discussing what's been learned.

The important thing is to identify and build your tribe quickly. These are the ones who will help you lead the work. Perhaps you need an email campaign. Ideally, you want that communication coming from the CEO. The purpose is to demonstrate how important the work is and to invite people who desire to be directly involved.

Create the right mix of individuals.

Your next propelling action is to create the right mix of people in your tribe. This mix should include individuals with position, power, expertise, and credibility. Make sure your tribe includes top leaders. At least one of the leaders should be from the executive level—meaning, the chief executive officer, perhaps the chief human resources officer, or the chief talent officer. It could be your employee resource group leaders or leaders from environmental, social and governance (ESG) or corporate and social responsibility (CSR). Your tribe of allies should contain a mix of individuals from all levels of the organization, starting at the top.

Determine your DEI governance structure.

Next, you will need to organize your tribe, which means a DEI governance structure is needed. This structure should have clear operating guidelines for getting the work done. It will also help you identify needs and gaps, as well as any overlaps in your DEI rollout. Knowing who is responsible for what also minimizes conflict and confusion within the tribe.

Below is an example of a DEI governance structure I helped to develop with one of my clients. They were a small company of a few hundred employees and very new to DEI work, so we kept the structure simple. But it will likely—and should—evolve over time.

In the immediate, the goal was to first determine who would provide strategic leadership for the work. In this case, it was the human resources director. I advised the client that at some point, they will need to have serious discussions about hiring a CDO. But at this point in their journey, it made sense to have the HR manager provide leadership for this effort.

Second, I helped them develop a deeper understanding and commitment around top leadership's role in the work. (Outlined below are the specific roles and tasks top leadership should be responsible for.)

We then focused on the next layer of leaders and DEI allies who would be responsible for supporting and implementing the strategic roadmap. Again, within this context, this group included the HR director, who provided strategic leadership, plus department heads and other DEI allies across the organization. We called this group an action council because they would play a significant role in the execution of the plan. Note that this is different from a DEI Advisory Council, which many organizations form. An advisory council typically provides advice or suggestions about DEI strategy, but an action council executes on that strategy.

DEI GOVERNANCE STRUCTURE

DEI Executive Council	DEI Action Council
Members: CEO and top executive team, HR director	Members: Department heads, HR director, and other DEI allies across the organization
Roles + Tasks:	
Defines the DEI vision for the organization and determines what success looks like.	**Roles + Tasks:**
	Supports and facilitates execution of the DEI strategic roadmap.
Supports the development and implementation of the DEI strategic roadmap.	Makes recommendations on how to implement and execute the DEI strategic roadmap.
Establishes the climate and culture for DEI work.	Champions others to engage in the DEI work.
Ensures adequate resources.	Models inclusive leadership behaviors.
Removes barriers from the process and work.	Meeting cadence: Monthly
Regularly communicates the DEI vision.	
Models inclusive leadership behaviors.	
Meeting cadence: Monthly	

As you determine your governance structure, be thoughtful about the distinctions between action and advisory councils and the significant role of language. Most importantly, determine a governance structure that fits your journey and context and has clear and realistic roles, tasks, and operating guidelines for getting the work done.

Equip your team with vision, resources, and tools.
The final action in building a tribe is making sure everyone is properly equipped. This includes sharing the vision and providing the resources and tools necessary for accomplishing the work. In practice, this looks like:

- Communicating a clear vision and expectations for roles.

- Providing training that develops the team's skills as change leaders.

- Meeting regularly (monthly) to ensure alignment of goals.

- Addressing any challenges that arise.

The governance structure will be your written resource that explains roles and responsibilities and guides the process. The initial training may include having the tribe participate in the DEI Propel course or something similar. We'll discuss this more in Step 5, but additional training will likely be needed and should be determined by an assessment of the strengths and weaknesses of the team and the overall skills needed to move the work forward.

Early on, the tribe should meet at least once a month, and potentially biweekly. Once you gain traction, you may determine a meeting cadence that requires meeting less frequently but often enough to keep the momentum going and manage accountability.

WAYS TO STRUCTURE YOUR DEI TRIBE

One of my clients was struggling with contextualizing the work within their organization. They did not have a CDO. Instead, they had a DEI Council. But the council was not clear about who had which roles and responsibilities. As a consequence, the group was well intended but dysfunctional. It wasn't clear who was responsible for providing strategic leadership around the work. Was it the council? Was it HR? This is one of many reasons building and effectively structuring your DEI tribe is so important.

Above, we looked at an example of a DEI tribe governance structure. Here are some additional insights into the thought process and actions for structuring an effective tribe. But first, know this: there are multiple ways to structure your tribe. It's up to you or whoever the strategic DEI leader is to identify the type of structure that will work best for your organization. At a minimum, consider these steps when establishing your structure.

Identify goals for your DEI tribe.

What problem are you trying to solve? Use the answer to this question to guide structuring your team. Make sure you consider who has the necessary relationships and influence to meet this goal. The key is to be strategic in selecting those capable of solving the problem, even if they do not have a background in DEI. One study revealed that only 28 percent of organizations hold their C-Suite executives accountable for DEI strategy progress.[2] To build a strategy, there must be a specific goal in mind. This begins with the goals for the tribe. What are you hoping to achieve? What problems will your tribe address?

Be clear on the roles and responsibilities of each person within your DEI tribe.

Who is responsible for what? Again, clarity about expected roles and responsibilities helps to reduce confusion and conflict within the tribe. It also allows individuals to contribute in their areas of strength while simultaneously becoming better equipped. Part of your role as a leader is to equip them and upskill them to support the work.

Reflect and Act

Thinking through the need to build a DEI tribe, take some time to answer the following questions and prompts. Do this before moving on to the next step.

1. **Reflect.** What type of DEI governance structure, if any, is in place at your organization? Is it the best structure to move the DEI work forward? What adjustments might you need to make?

2. **Act.** Develop or update your DEI governance structure for your DEI tribe.

KEY TAKEAWAYS

- Building a DEI tribe is an essential step in developing and implementing a DEI strategic roadmap.

- Don't just vet for passion. Make sure the people in your tribe have influence across the organization and a strong commitment to the work.

- Organize by building a strong governance structure that is clear about roles and responsibilities.

- Be prepared to upskill them. They are not DEI experts.

Step 3

MAP THE ROUTE

THERE'S AN OLD saying: "Don't enter a maze without a map." Though the saying's origins are unknown, the advice proves invaluable on the DEI journey.

Just like a corn maze, DEI work is full of twists, turns, and unknowns. The journey is further complicated by the number of individuals that must pass through the winding labyrinth to make progress. And yet, like a corn maze, this is all normal. Even so, to make real progress, you need direction. You need a plan.

Shawn Stolworthy, whose company designs and builds corn mazes across the United States and Canada, says that when going through a maze, "Figure out where north, south, east and west are before you go in."[1] Basic directional awareness can help you find your way through a tortuous, branching path, even when your ability to see is limited by cornstalks as high as fourteen feet. Stolworthy goes on to say, "To feel the full range of pride, relief and joy upon successfully exiting a maze, it helps to first allow yourself time to be adrift." Although you never fully exit DEI work in the same way you'd exit a corn maze, the pride, relief, and joy you'll experience from the hard work and successes you meet along the journey will make the challenge more than worth it.

Even so, a clear roadmap significantly increases your level of success and impact. Now that you've built your tribe and have a solid group of allies to help lead the work, it's time to determine the actual DEI plan for your organization and get started.

CREATE A VISION

First, you need to create a clear DEI vision. This will serve as the guiding star for your strategic roadmap.

Your vision needs to be clear, not complicated. It should be straightforward. Another way of thinking about the clarity of your DEI vision is that if it takes you more than five minutes to explain it, it's too complicated. Everyone across the organization should understand and be able to articulate what it means. Eventually, they will also need to understand their role in helping to make the vision become a reality.

If you don't already have a DEI vision statement or it's outdated, you'll want to work collaboratively with your DEI tribe to develop it. Make sure the vision doesn't just focus on numbers but specifies the organization's direction. Some vision statements are longer than others. There are no hard and fast rules on length. What's important is that it be understandable and motivate people to want to get behind it.

Here are a few examples of some good DEI vision statements:

> The future of work is equitable and inclusive. Indeed is working to close the opportunity gap by reducing bias and removing barriers for hundreds of millions of job seekers worldwide.
>
> —INDEED.COM[2]

> NIKE, Inc. is building more equitable and inclusive practices to empower our current 80,000 employees and create the workforce of the future.
>
> —NIKE[3]

We actively seek diversity, boldly pursue equity, and consciously promote inclusion to create a sense of belonging for all people.

—DELTA AIRLINES[4]

Building diverse teams to serve a diverse platform. On the Uber platform, a staggering number of different people interact with one another across our 19 million trips a day. We need to build our products and run our business in a way that effectively serve the diverse communities who use our products. That means it's essential for our workforce internally to reflect the diversity of the communities in which we operate and hire, and for us to cultivate an environment where that diversity thrives and where people feel they belong and can contribute to our shared success.

By making gradual and sustainable changes over time, Uber has rebuilt the foundation from the bottom up and completely reshaped our culture. Five years later, we are already seeing how diversity is making us stronger and enabling us to create a more equitable and inclusive environment to move the world for the better.

—UBER[5]

Think of your DEI vision statement as the destination for the work your tribe and organization are headed to reach. What place do you want to reach with this work?

CREATE A STRATEGIC ROADMAP

After defining your DEI vision, you'll need to create a strategic roadmap for its implementation. What route will you take to arrive at your desired destination?

Here's a key point: Your strategy needs to be measurable and should align with the overall business strategy of your organization. As mentioned earlier, DEI is far more than an HR topic or issue. It should be core to the design and execution of the overall business strategy. It should be embedded in daily activities across the organization. There should be alignment with your environmental, social, and governance efforts and your corporate and social responsibility efforts.

As you begin to develop your roadmap, be sure to make this part of the process collaborative. Take the time you need to collect any additional relevant data. Then solicit feedback from other DEI leaders and allies across the organization. If you're developing this plan for your department or area, seek feedback from your team.

Now, there are several key components to the roadmap. We'll unpack each of them in detail. But for now I'll say that you want to prioritize strategies, actions, and KPIs. These should be outcome-based and data-driven based on the greatest opportunities and employee feedback. They should also build on the head and heart data we discussed in Step 1.

I use three questions to guide this part of the work:

1. What data is informing the decisions and strategies around DEI?

2. Where do you see the biggest gaps and opportunities?

3. What perceived gaps and opportunities do your employees see?

I draw specific attention to questions two and three when working with teams, as I have found that what a leader or manager sees as a gap may not be the same gap identified by employees. Achieving alignment requires clear communication and feedback to ensure the correct challenges are being addressed in the implementation of the strategic roadmap. In sum, the strategy for successfully routing your map will be driven by your ability to incorporate employee feedback and identify the greatest opportunities.

So, how do we do this? Let's break down the six specific steps necessary to create the roadmap and how we use the data (employee feedback and the greatest opportunities) to inform the plan. You'll see that I have used talent acquisition as an example of a strategic focus area and the flow through the six steps.

DEI STRATEGIC ROADMAP

Organization:

DEI Vision Statement:

| **Strategic Areas of Focus** | **Outcomes** | **Priorities** |

- Talent Acquisition

- Increased number of diverse applicants in the talent pool

- Analyze data to assess opportunities and pain points
- Diversify sourcing channels
- Insure diverse interview panels
- Unconcious bias training
- Review recruitment process
- Disaggregate demo-graphic data to identify diversity disparities in who is being hired
- Review job criteria for exclusionary language and unnecessary job requirements
- Be open to nontraditional backgrounds

| **Key Performance Indicators** | **Facilitator** | **Timeline** |

- Diversity in applicants increased by X percent
- Diversity of candidate slate presented to hiring manager increased by X percent
- Invested in an inclusive language guidance or AI tool to manage bias in job ads

- Chief Diversity Officer
- Department Head
- Human Resources

- Quarter 1
  * Increased diversity in applicants

Step 1: Identify your strategic areas of focus

The first step toward creating your DEI strategic roadmap is identifying your strategic areas of focus. What does this mean? It means identifying the specific areas you are going to target to effectively move the work forward. You might ask, "How do I decide what areas to focus on?" There are a couple of ways to think about this.

In an ideal scenario, your organization has done a comprehensive DEI needs assessment and you have hard data to inform where you need to focus your efforts. However, not every organization has made this level of investment. If that's your reality, don't worry. There are other ways to seek out helpful data. Start by taking a deep dive into your organization's or department's diversity data. The following questions will bring the needed areas of focus into clear view, based on that diversity data:

- What is the data telling you about diverse representation (race, gender, disability, sexual orientation, generational differences, etc.) or lack of it in the organization or your department?

- Does your organization facilitate employee engagement surveys? What does that data tell you?

- What are your retention and promotion rates?

- What cultural groups are staying, and which ones are leaving? Why?

- We know women in the United States are only paid 83 cents for every dollar men make. That number drops to 70 cents for Black women and

65 cents for Latina women.[6] What are the pay equity gaps in your organization or department?

• What other patterns and themes do you see?

These questions will get you started, and point you toward the kind of data you need to inform your areas of focus, though I'm confident there will be other areas related to DEI you also need to consider. In their book *Inclusalytics: How Diversity, Equity, and Inclusion Leaders Use Data to Drive Their Work*, authors Victoria Mattingly, Sertrice Grice, and Allison Goldstein provide some excellent evidence-based insights on how to use data to inform your DEI strategy.

Once you have collected your data, use it to prioritize your strategic areas of focus based on the greatest opportunities and employee feedback. As you ask yourself these questions, think beyond the surface and symptoms. In other words, look for the root causes.

You could ask these questions: Why and where are we having a problem attracting and/or retaining diverse talent? Is it because we've bought into the myth that we can't find diverse talent? Is it because we're seeking diverse talent in the wrong places? Is it because our interview process might be biased? Is it because the language in job descriptions favors certain cultural groups and detracts others? Is it because we want diverse representation but aren't committed to creating an inclusive culture? Do we expect people from under-represented groups to assimilate, rather than being themselves? Are we afraid to offend or upset the dominant group or the resistors? Part of the process of prioritizing strategic areas of focus not only includes an assessment of what the data is saying, but also a hard and honest analysis of why the data is what it is.

Google provides a strong real-world example of determining strategic areas of focus. In their 2022 Diversity Annual Report, Chief Diversity Officer Melonie Parker highlights five of Google's strategic areas of focus: (1) hiring, (2) retention and progression, (3) representation, (4) flexibility, and (5) belonging and innovation.[7] These may not be your organization's areas of focus, and your organization may not be as far along in the journey as Google, but this list can at least help stimulate your thinking.

I suggest you choose 3-4 strategic areas of focus to start. While identifying them, make sure you're collaborating on it with your DEI tribe. Do not do it in isolation.

Step 2: Determine outcomes

Next, you must determine what outcomes you want to achieve and how they will support your strategic areas of focus. For example, if you focus on talent acquisition as a strategic area of focus, your primary outcome might be to increase the number of diverse applicants in the talent pool.

And yes, it's not only okay to include goals; it's necessary. We set specific goals and targets for other areas like finance and sales. Why not DEI? If you don't measure it, it's not a strategy. Developing a DEI strategic roadmap without clear metrics is a huge miss and will 100 percent undermine your efforts at having a sustainable impact in your organization. We see this happen all the time. Don't let this be your narrative.

But what if you get pushback? For example, someone might ask, "Is it really fair to do these things for certain cultural groups, such as African Americans, and not others? Wouldn't that be perceived as reverse discrimination?" I once was asked these exact questions in a strategy session with a team of white executives. One leader added, "And why do we need to add quotas? That's just going to make other employees cringe!"

As you develop your outcomes and priorities and work to address inequities inside your organization, you may also encounter these kinds of questions. You might even struggle with them yourself. This is where understanding history and the data comes into play. The broader facts are clear. African Americans have been systematically disadvantaged in the United States for years. As a country, we still have a lot of work and catching up to do.

Let me offer a few questions for consideration around this:

- Do you have strong representation and decision-making power of African Americans at all levels of the organization?

- Do they receive equitable promotions, opportunities, and compensation?

- Are you creating space for your Black employees to share their lived experiences in the organization?

- Do they feel included and like they belong?

- What does your data tell you?

If you can answer yes with supporting data to most of these questions, you are well on your way to promoting a racially equitable workplace. If you can't, determine the gaps and work to close them.

Your strategy may need more robust metrics. These questions can apply to Black, Brown, gay, differently abled, and any other marginalized group that has been disadvantaged by unfair decisions and systems. Remind yourself and others that fairness requires special attention and specific actions to support those who are otherwise treated unjustly by the system. It's about creating equitable opportunities for everyone.

This doesn't mean we neglect wisdom or legal counsel. We fully understand that according to Title VII of the Civil Rights Act, it is illegal to consider any candidate's or employee's race—even with the intention of creating a more diverse, equitable, and inclusive workforce—in any employment decision. This would include hiring quotas.

At the same time, according to the law, even after the SCOTUS decision, gender and race-conscious hiring practices *are permitted*, assuming there is evidence of inequities and/or imbalance in attracting, retaining, and promoting underrepresented groups, such as females, people of color, or veterans. In most organizations, if we honor the truth, these inequities aren't hard to find.

Step 3: Determine priorities

Now that we've identified outcomes, we need to determine priorities, which are the outcomes-based activities and inclusive behaviors we need to do to accomplish the outcomes. To elaborate on this using the previous example, if you set an outcome to increase the number of diverse applicants, one priority might be to disaggregate demographic data and use it to identify diversity-related disparities, such as race, gender, or being differently abled, when it comes to who is being hired. Another might be to review job criteria for exclusionary language and unnecessary job requirements, and to be open to nontraditional backgrounds.

Clear priorities are important because our goal in DEI work is to move from priorities to achieving our outcomes. Priorities are actions only, not rooted in anything long term. Outcomes, on the other hand, connect to an intended plan. This is what we want.

Additional examples can include everything from diversifying sourcing channels to ensuring diverse interview panels to unconscious bias training.

Step 4: Determine key performance indicators (KPIs)

In addition to outcomes and priorities, you need to identify key performance indicators (KPIs). Customize your KPIs by being as specific as possible. This helps you measure whether you are making progress. For example, your KPIs for talent acquisition could be that the diversity in applicants increased by X percent, the diversity of the candidate slate presented to the hiring manager increased by X percent, or that you've invested in an inclusive language guidance or AI tool, such as Textio, to manage bias in job ads and increase your diversity pipeline. Follow this same pattern and process for each of your strategic areas of focus. Your KPIs should become more substantive over time and should be measuring behavior and systems change.

Step 5: Determine facilitators

As mentioned earlier, while someone, such as the CDO, director of diversity, or a department head, should provide strategic leadership for the DEI work of your organization, the work should ultimately be a shared responsibility. It's important at this point to think about which individuals will help facilitate and implement the roadmap. Go back to your DEI governance structure. Will it be someone from your DEI tribe? Will it be the director of HR, a department head, or another ally in the organization? A combination of all of these? Begin to think about and write down who will take on these tasks. Just as important, think about how you will hold them accountable and what support they might need from you.

Step 6: Establish a timeline

I can't reiterate enough that DEI work is a journey. You never fully arrive, but you can make progress—and you need to be intentional about how and when to expect to see results. Establishing clear timelines is a critical component of your roadmap.

Initially, you should view and develop your strategic roadmap as a two-year plan that will expand and improve beyond the two years. You'll also likely adjust it during those two years, and that's perfectly fine. Setting realistic timelines for tasks is just as important as the tasks themselves. While you want to be aggressive with the work and stretch yourself and the organization, you don't want to establish timelines that are overly ambitious or unrealistic. For example, if you to try to revamp your talent acquisition process and systems, facilitate unconscious bias training with all hiring managers, and redesign your onboarding process all in the first three to six months, that might be too much. At the same time, do set stretch goals and commit to real change sooner versus later.

Begin to prioritize and break down the actions for each of the strategic areas of focus over a two-year period. Think first about what will be accomplished in Year 1 and then Year 2. Then go back and break the years down into quarters. What will you accomplish in Q1, Q2, Q3, and Q4? Breaking it down in this way will help reduce feeling overwhelmed as the work is implemented. Again, be flexible and willing to adapt as you go.

FINALIZE YOUR DEI ROADMAP

I bet you're thinking this requires a lot of thought and work! You're right. The good news is you're using a research-based framework and leading practices to build this, so you're set up to develop and implement a strategy that guarantees lasting results.

One final point: I strongly recommend linking your KPIs to accountability to achieve sustainable results. In practice, this looks like connecting them to performance reviews, promotions, and professional development. Another way is to assign a goal to each person's job description, and then to take it a step deeper and tie those goals to performance reviews. This goes back to the idea of "calling in versus calling out," which is about accountability and the expectation that everyone participates.

Now, this isn't a situation of "If you don't meet these goals, you're fired." But it is about the expectation that just as employees develop in their areas of expertise or discipline, they are also expected to grow in cultural intelligence and commitment to diversity, equality, and inclusion.

In these performance reviews, it's not about attacking but about establishing at least one goal related to DEI. You might say, "Let's have a conversation about it. How is it going? What can I do to support you? What other resources do you need to be successful?" When you tie DEI measures to accountability and performance goals, it becomes more real to everyone across the organization.

Other examples of DEI performance goals might be:

- Linking executive compensation to DEI performance metrics.

- Requiring managers to pull from a diverse pool of candidates for every posted job position.

- Requiring department heads to participate in unconscious bias training.

- Building in an annual review of bias in policies and practices by HR leaders and department heads.

Reflect and Act

As you can see, this step is the real meat of this book. It's where you need to spend most of your energy to develop the strategic roadmap that will guide all your efforts.

So far, we've identified the first three steps in making DEI work operational. You've created the case for "now, not later" efforts and buy-in. You've developed your DEI tribe and governance structure. Now you're putting that clear, concise plan together with prioritized actions based on data. Before moving to the next steps, take some time to pause, reflect, and act.

1. **Reflect.** What data has been used to inform your current DEI strategy or efforts? What will be your strategic areas of focus? How will you measure success?

2. **Act.** Develop your DEI strategic roadmap by working through all six steps outlined on page 66.

KEY TAKEAWAYS

- Your DEI vision needs to be clear, not complicated.

- The data-driven and outcome-based strategic roadmap must support the vision.

- The DEI strategic roadmap should align with the overall business strategy.

- Every strategy on the roadmap should have metrics attached to it.

- DEI is a shared responsibility. Metrics should be designated to create accountability across the organization.

Step 4

SHARE YOUR DEI PLAN

I ONCE WAS BROUGHT into a large technology company to perform a DEI organizational audit. It didn't take long for employee feedback to indicate a number of areas in need of attention and action. When I shared these findings with leadership, some senior managers immediately became defensive. They responded with "But we're doing that" and "People just don't listen." I shared even more feedback, which led to similar sentiments being echoed again: "We're addressing that" and "We took care of that when..." I shared the feedback calmly, without emotion and with the reminder that it came directly from the employees, not from me.

Needless to say, the employees' feedback compared with the leadership's efforts revealed a significant gap in perception concerning the organization's DEI progress. It also exposed a serious gap in communication. The leaders were doing what they thought was right to address the issues, but they'd failed to communicate their intentions, actions, and successes to their employees.

This wasn't the first time I'd encountered this scenario. It might even mirror what you have experienced when you've provided not-so-positive employee feedback to leadership or when you see a yawning chasm between leadership's view of progress and success versus everyone else's perception in the organization.

KEYS TO COMMUNICATING WELL

In the first three steps, we identified the urgency for DEI work, created a tribe of individuals to guide the work, and developed the first iteration of our strategic roadmap. The final step in Phase 1 is to communicate that roadmap to others. We've put in the hard work to develop it. Now it's time to share the vision across the organization.

Our DEI plan should never be a secret. However, wide understanding can only occur when it's effectively communicated. Just as we need to get buy-in to commit to the work, we need to get buy-in to implement the work.

Unfortunately, effective communication is one of the greatest weaknesses in many organizations when it comes to DEI work. Having a vision is one thing; communicating it is another. These two aspects are connected, but they're different tasks in the process. Let's consider some of the key assumptions related to both.

It needs to be user friendly.

Sometimes, when we've worked on something for a while, it's hard to step back and summarize any of its concepts. This can easily happen when it comes to a DEI vision and roadmap. I mentioned in Step 3 that our vision should be simple and effectively communicated in less than five minutes. Think about creating an even shorter summary—thirty seconds or less—that you could use in casual conversation to prompt a longer discussion. It's also important to broadcast this message across the organization broadly and often.

It needs to be repeated.

In his book *Leading Change,* John Kotter notes, "The real power of a vision is unleashed only when most of those involved in an enterprise...have a common understanding of its goals and direction."[1] He further adds that new ideas sink in deeply only after they've been heard numerous times. In addition to being communicated broadly, the vision and roadmap should be communicated often and consistently. Everyone from the CEO to the frontline workers to the back office staff should be able to articulate the company's DEI vision.

If our DEI vision is discussed thoroughly within our guiding tribe but not shared openly with the entire organization regularly, then our strategy will not be effective. If everyone doesn't know what's going on, what the priorities are, or what's happening, then sustainable DEI will never be achieved. It takes everyone.

It needs to be consistent.

Another important layer of sharing your DEI vision rests in the consistency of your messaging. All leaders and DEI tribe members should utilize the same language to communicate the vision. This will eliminate confusion about the vision and provide an opportunity for employees to hear the same information from multiple sources, offer feedback, and ask questions. Reinforcement with consistency of messaging also supports everyone working toward the same goal and understanding.

It needs to be modeled.

The final and most important factor in communicating the DEI vision and roadmap is modeling appropriate behaviors. Leadership and the DEI tribe should demonstrate culturally intelligent and inclusive behaviors. One of the fastest ways to undermine our DEI effort is for our actions to be contrary to our vision. Remember, we started at the beginning by emphasizing that DEI is all about change—changing individual behaviors and changing systems. The leadership and tribe's behaviors and actions should model the vision and plan. This modeling can be demonstrated by a diverse leadership team. It can also be observed when leadership actively listens to feedback and is willing to engage in uncomfortable conversations.

During a consulting session with a client, one of the leaders asked me how leadership's behaviors can impact the 25 percent of resistors, otherwise known as the "sticky middle." I explained that some people resist simply because leadership isn't walking the talk. Inconsistency and misaligned actions are often the culprits that keep that 25 percent from actively engaging in DEI work. This is added confirmation that the guiding team needs to walk out the plan, to really live what's being said in terms of the vision.

Propelling Actions

We've built a case for communicating the DEI vision and roadmap throughout the organization. Now it's time to operationalize that work with strategy and action. How can we communicate what we're envisioning, saying, and doing with our DEI work?

In sum, there are two primary strategies for sharing the vision: using every possible avenue and modeling the way. Here are specific ways you can operationalize these strategies.

Use every avenue.

Think about and use every possible avenue to communicate your DEI vision and roadmap. It's going to take this approach to broaden the reach of the message. Employing various avenues to communicate the vision and strategy will allow employees at all levels of the organization to be informed. Using multiple avenues in culturally intelligent ways also ensures that various learning styles, cultural values, and language differences are accommodated.

Using every avenue possible means communicating the DEI vision in multiple forums. A few are listed below:

- Direct communication from CDO/CEO

- Company newsletters

- Town halls

- Department and team meetings

- One-on-one meetings

- Performance reviews

It's important that all of these spaces are psychologically safe, and create room for employees to process the information, offer important ideas, and ask critical questions.

As you do this, ensure the messages are consistent. Also be sure to create space and opportunities for employees to process, respond, and ask questions. And then, of course, be sure to keep repeating these actions.

Model the way.

Senior leaders and DEI champions should not only teach the behavior, but also demonstrate it in their own walk. This can be done in five ways:

1. Create and implement a leadership development program with action plans.

2. Communicate leadership's plans and actions to employees.

3. Assign top leaders as executive sponsors to high-potential employees from underrepresented populations.

4. Connect DEI goals to a leader's performance goals.

5. Take action after you receive feedback (solicited and unsolicited).

Our key strategies of using every avenue and modeling the behaviors are supported by specific actions. By pursuing these kinds of actions, you will have a greater likelihood of employees responding favorably to the news about the DEI strategic roadmap.

REFLECT AND ACT

Think about spreading the word about your organization's DEI efforts. How will you ensure it's done clearly and repeatedly? Remember to answer honestly!

1. **Reflect.** How is your organization's current DEI Strategic Roadmap being communicated? How do you know if people understand it?

2. **Act.** Develop or revise your DEI communications plan to include the strategies highlighted in Step 4.

KEY TAKEAWAYS

• A clear DEI vision should take less than five minutes to explain.

• You need a formal DEI communications plan to communicate the vision and strategy throughout the organization.

• DEI communications should reach every level of the organization.

• The DEI vision and roadmap can be communicated in several culturally intelligent ways. Use them all.

• The most effective ways to perpetuate sustainable DEI practices is by modeling and demonstrating inclusive actions through leadership and the DEI tribe.

PHASE 2
INTRODUCING NEW DEI PRACTICES

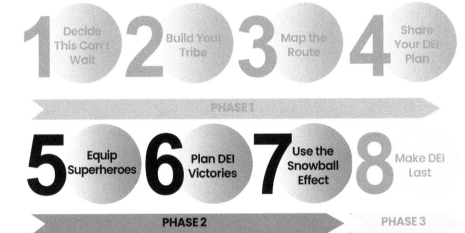

Step 5

EQUIP SUPERHEROES

I N THIS CHAPTER, we're going to talk about equipping the superheroes in your organization because a team of superheroes—not just a single person—will actively lead the work. Why superheroes? I mean, isn't calling them superheroes a bit exaggerated? Yes, if you're thinking about the ones in the movies. But here, we're talking about real-life superheroes, those who are passionate about DEI work and willing to sustain the effort, even when it gets hard and uncomfortable. These superheroes are part of your DEI tribe, and they need to be trained and upskilled to engage in, or facilitate, courageous conversations.

To be a real hero, passion alone isn't enough. These superheroes will need to be equipped to implement DEI in their areas or departments. This requires them to have the right tools and resources. In addition to demonstrating the behaviors that support the work, they will also support the removal of systems and structures that are barriers to your DEI goals.

So, where do we start? We start with leadership.

Every leader or manager will need some refreshing, and often they'll need some training. To initiate these efforts, go back to your DEI strategic roadmap. Take a look at the individuals to whom you assigned tasks. They will need to be equipped and supported as well. Eventually, everyone in the organization will need to engage in learning and development,

but individuals at the top—your DEI tribe and other allies—
should lead the work.

Changing Individual Behaviors

I've been grateful to consistently receive high marks on
training programs that I facilitate. I believe this is for at least
three reasons.

First, before I agree to facilitate a session, I insist that the
client understand that a training program is not a DEI strategy.
Instead, it should be part of a larger and thoughtful plan that
is inclusive of everything we are talking about in this book.
With that said, learning and development is a very important part of the process. It's one of the key places where your
organization has the opportunity to change and nurture individual and team behaviors that consistently support, and never
undermine, the DEI efforts.

Second, my training always has a research-based foundation,
meaning that the principles and concepts I share are based
on evidence that, if implemented properly, work and produce
lasting results. At the same time, the trainings are interactive
and focus on providing participants with practical strategies
and actionable items they can implement immediately.

Third, I emphasize the importance of testing for efficacy.
In other words, how can we ensure that this training actually changes and produces behaviors that support the organization's DEI goals that are highlighted on the roadmap? This
is an important question because significant research suggests
that to impact behaviors, there must be additional interven-
tions, support, and resources made available *after* a training.[1]
For example, if you conduct a training on cultural intelligence,
perhaps in the following weeks, you can offer participants

weekly tips on how to become more culturally intelligent. Or you can discuss the topic in a staff meeting, asking staff members how the processes of implementing their strategies or action items are coming along and if they need any support from you. Participants can complete the post-CQ Assessment to measure if there CO has improved. You can also build the discussion into individual performance reviews. These are a few examples of how you can build in accountability and increase the likelihood that employees are practicing the needed behaviors. No doubt you'll create some of your own.

CREATE INCLUSIVE ENVIRONMENTS

When my daughter was in elementary school, she sometimes wore what I considered mismatched clothes. One morning, she put on one polka-dot sock and one striped sock of completely different colors.

"You know those don't match, right?" I said.

"Says who?" she replied. "Who made that decision?"

I carry that response of innocence and clarity with me to this day. I remember thinking at the time, "That's a fantastic question—who said, and why?" Someone, somewhere decided everything should match, but whatever socks my daughter wanted to wear had zero to do with her ability to go to school and learn. Our differing perspectives over matching clothes ended that day.

I share this story often when working with organizations on strategy. It's a perfect example of how traditional policies and practices can create unnecessary limitations, far beyond the color of our socks, especially for certain cultural groups.

For example, LinkedIn and Dove teamed up to create more inclusive and equitable spaces for Black hair in the workplace.

Why? Because according to the 2023 CROWN Act Research Study,[2] Black women's hair is 2.5 times more likely to be perceived as unprofessional. As a consequence, approximately 66 percent of Black women change their hair for a job interview.

This unfortunate reality is just one example of why the conversation around professional presence is so important. It also raises the question: Who gets to decide what is professional? And how do we know when we've crossed the line of forced assimilation, discouraging people from being themselves in perfectly professional ways? How can we be sure we don't support systems and practices that, while "traditional," actively undermine our claims to desire an inclusive work environment?

Below are three of the biggest threats to creating an inclusive organization and what you can do about each.

Threat #1: Expectations dictated by the dominant culture's values

The dominant culture is the shared culture of the largest and usually most powerful group in an organization. Those who have status and privilege position these values to establish policies and organizational routines based on how they define professionalism. This might include a requirement for men to wear a suit or tie or saying that certain types of jewelry are too flashy for men or women. Often, individual expression or the cultural values and heritage of underrepresented groups are dismissed as "unprofessional" when, in fact, they have absolutely no impact on work or our work's outcomes.

So, what can you do about this? First, reflect on who decides what professional means in your organization. Is the process inclusive? Are diverse voices considered? Invite a diverse team to express the organizational culture by welcoming individual styles and celebrating cultural differences, including cultural dress and heritage. For example, demonstrate support for women of color by signing the Crown Act petition.[3] When it comes to gender diversity, make sure dress policies are as gender neutral as possible. Also ensure that differently abled or neurodiverse employees are not hit with professional presence practices that do not offer reasonable accommodations.

Threat #2: Expectations unrelated to the individual's ability to do their job

Historically, tattoos have been frowned upon in many workplaces. Yet today, almost half—yes, half!—of millennials in the United States have at least one tattoo,[4] and many of them are regarded as art to be displayed. This example exposes how some organizations can have unrealistic and biased thinking about things that have little to no influence on an employee's performance. As tattoos have become more prevalent, employers are wise to become more accepting of them. Most have discovered that rarely does a person's tattoos have anything to do with the employee's ability to do their job.

What can you do about this threat? Hold yourself and others who make hiring and promotion decisions accountable for staying laser focused on the requirements necessary for your employees to do their jobs—period. Then supplement that commitment by creating an environment that allows them to do their work while being their authentic selves and reflecting their cultural heritage. Even the US military lifted[5] its "25 percent rule," a policy that prevented military personnel from tattooing more than 25 percent of their body.

Threat #3: Policies and practices that create equity gaps across the organization

Individuals who don't "fit" with the mainstream look, language, or behaviors risk being confined to entry-level positions with limited opportunities for promotion and development. If they have a nose piercing or dress in ways that express their transgender identity, they may quickly experience being marginalized and disadvantaged. Over time, inequities are created that lead to only certain individuals or cultural groups being represented at an organization's highest level or even among middle management positions.

Here's what you can do about this threat. Take a hard look at those individuals across your organization who have not been provided opportunities for advancement. Do you see any patterns and themes? If there are legitimate issues where professionalism is lacking, support those individuals by providing training and coaching.

It is completely appropriate to expect employees to demonstrate they care about their appearance, their communication, and how they present themselves to others in culturally intelligent ways. At the same time, those who make decisions about organizational policies related to professional behavior need to consider the impact on a diverse employee base. If an organization has five or six ethnic or historic cultures represented among its employees yet most upper management and leadership roles are filled by people from just one tradition, the organization's culture may be troubled.

Companies often miss out on talent because of policies that exclude qualified individuals based on characteristics that have no impact on their performance ability. Take this back to the story of my daughter's socks and how her attire had no impact on her school performance. When this happens in organizations, it directly contradicts claims of commitment to diversity, equity, and inclusion.

Traditional policies and practices, which are often created by a dominant culture, keep us stuck in the corporate mud and prevent real change. They also often have the greatest impact on the equity part of the DEI equation. This is because, historically, it has been the creation of systems that benefit certain groups and disadvantage others and create disparities. And unfortunately, many of those inequitable systems are still intact. Your DEI allies, depending on their role and influence in the organization, should lead or support efforts to adjust or completely remove systems, policies, and practices that form barriers to creating a DEI organization. Your organization should also create new systems that support the work. Another just as important part of creating superheroes is creating psychologically safe spaces and supporting them through social justice issues.

CREATING NEW SYSTEMS

I feel as if I'm continually harping about system changes, but they are fundamental to our DEI work. W. Edwards Deming, the father of continuous quality improvement, in 1982 claimed in his book *Out of the Crisis* that 94 percent of workplace issues are systemic.[6] I believe he's right. DEI is no exception. The work and research of past and present-day scholars, such as Roosevelt Thomas, Ibram Kendi, and Isabel Wilkerson, remind us that the history of America was built on ideas and systems that favored certain groups and disenfranchised others. These systems are alive and well today—and they are steeped inside our organizations, even if we do not instantly recognize them.

All of the systems, policies, and practices of your organization should support the DEI vision and roadmap. Review
every stage of the employee life cycle, from talent acquisition to onboarding to promotion and development, with an
eye toward policies and practices and ask, "Does this policy
or practice serve as a benefit or barrier to our DEI efforts?"
For the areas that are misaligned, create new policies. Unlike
with clothes and appearance, this is where matching matters.
Your routines and systems should match and further your DEI
vision. In addition, everyone in the organization should feel
safe to challenge, in appropriate ways, systems that go against
the DEI work.

Psychological safety

If people don't feel safe to speak up and be themselves, they
won't feel like a superhero. In fact, they'll feel more like a vil-
lain. On the contrary, when employees feel comfortable asking
for help, sharing suggestions informally, or challenging the
status quo without fear of negative consequences, organizations are more likely to unlock the benefits of diversity and
adapt well to change.[7]

This is about creating a psychologically safe environment.
Psychological safety is defined as the belief that you won't be
punished for making a mistake or penalized for sharing perspectives based on lived experiences. The theory behind the
positive relationship between DEI and psychological safety is
far from new. However, Amy C. Edmondson, Harvard Business
School professor and author of *The Fearless Organization*, actually coined the phrase *team psychological safety* and argues
that emerging research is proving what many of us already
knew: that psychological safety is one of the keys to realizing
DEI efforts.[8]

Unfortunately, many employees don't feel safe in the workplace. This concern is multiplied for underrepresented groups. When a workplace is deemed psychologically safe, it makes space for deeper connections. Psychologically safe environments also yield higher levels of engagement, creativity, and performance.[9] This is not an easy task, but it should certainly be a goal.

Consider how your organization is doing when it comes to creating a psychologically safe space. What progress do you feel is being made? I especially appreciate Jodi-Ann Burey's TedX Talk on the myth of bringing your authentic self to work. She says, "Without accountability to examine these systems of bias and power, the call for authenticity fails."[10] If we are going to empower others to act, part of that empowerment includes ensuring the systems in place support their behaviors.

As you empower DEI superheroes in your organization, remember that some topics may evoke more tension and resistance than others. How often have you heard someone say, "Diversity is more than race!" I hear that sentiment often—okay, very often—when working with organizations. In fact, I've said it myself. Why? Because it's true. Diversity is a broad and inclusive term. Not only does it expand well beyond race, but it also includes invisible forms of diversity, such as disability, religion, and socioeconomic status.

However, we have to be careful. If this statement is used to scapegoat and minimize the role that race and racist systems play in the conversation and the work to create a more diverse, equitable, and inclusive work environment, that's problematic. These tough and courageous conversations are an essential part of the process of dismantling old, unhelpful systems, creating new systems, and creating a psychologically safe space for everyone.

There are several ways to encourage psychological safety at work. We previously discussed a number of them in Steps 1–4. Useful strategies include, for example, establishing and communicating a clear DEI vision, encouraging open communication, actively listening to employees, and responding in a timely manner when people do speak up to share ideas or concerns.

Social justice and the workplace

A few years back, I was at an event in New York City with several DEI leaders from across the United States. Our time together was rich with conversation and ideation. I facilitated some of the dialogue, beginning with my usual first question, which you may remember from the beginning of this book: "What's keeping you up at night?"

People didn't hesitate to share their thoughts. Comments flooded the room. One chief diversity officer shouted, "What's keeping me up at night is figuring out how to support my employees through social injustices." Heads bobbed in agreement all over the room.

I think no one working in this space, leaders and allies alike, would argue that 2020 and 2021 became the years in which social injustice was impossible to ignore and even unwise to try to avoid. Social issues were front and center in our homes, our schools, our congregations, and our workplaces, forcing leaders to adjust their DEI approach.

I understood this leader's challenge. And as I listened and looked around our gathering, it was clear others did too. When employees come into work after a particularly traumatic event, they do not have the luxury of leaving their trauma at the door.

There is no magic switch that turns off the impact of what's going on, especially if the incident hits close to home.

This idea of supporting employees through social injustices is a big deal. In fact, research from Gartner, an advisory and business insights company, indicates that 68 percent of employees "would consider quitting their current job and working with an organization with a stronger viewpoint on the social issues that matter most to them."[11] The same study found that "employees whose employer has taken a strong stance on current societal and cultural issues are twice as likely to report high job satisfaction."

If there is no space inside the organization for discussion around trauma events, or even an acknowledgment of them, it's hard for people to take seriously the organization's claimed commitment to the DEI work or its goals.

I imagine that just reading this has some readers feeling anxious. It's uncomfortable, for sure, and scary. Some worries drop in: "What if we say the wrong thing?" "What if things backfire?" I can't promise that you won't say some things wrong. Nor can I promise that you won't receive pushback. What I can tell you is that silence is never a good strategy. In fact, it makes us complicit. When something happens in the outside world that impacts a segment of our workplace's inside world, we don't want to "ghost" those who are most impacted. Underrepresented groups or those who have been historically marginalized or excluded don't have the privilege of opting out of uncomfortable circumstances. It's often part of their daily lived experiences, both inside and outside our organizations. To create real and transformational change, the work and the discomfort have to be shared. Everyone has to lean in. No one is exempt.

Simply put, organizations that take refuge in silence risk their ability to retain employees and attract new candidates, especially women, people of color, and the younger generation. Retention and attraction are both tied to the number of super-heroes and individuals that are available to propel DEI work forward.

In Step 1, we discussed at length the notion of calling people in to this work. Step 5 on this journey is about calling people in *and* empowering them to act on the DEI vision. Empowering means equipping them with the confidence and skills to help get the work done, both at the individual and systems level.

PROPELLING ACTIONS

I've shared several foundational practices and ideas for empow-ering superheroes and propelling our efforts at engaging others forward. Let's look at several ways to operationalize some of these thoughts and strategies.

Review current policies and practices.

The place to begin here is with an initial DEI assessment that becomes at least an annual practice. You'll also want to facili-tate quarterly systems reviews within each department with the help of your DEI allies, DEI council members, or depart-ment heads. Note that an important step here is to equip, via training, those DEI allies and department heads with the skills needed to facilitate those reviews.

Create new systems, policies, practices and routines that align with the vision.

Once you've completed the initial DEI assessment (also known as a DEI audit), you can use the data to inform system and policy change. Be sure to track sizeable data from different identities—especially underrepresented groups—and across different levels of the organization. Notice how the data aligns, or doesn't align, with items on your roadmap. This gives you the clear places to begin.

Encourage risk taking and inclusive ideas, activities, and actions.
We've talked quite a bit about the importance of perspective taking and creating psychologically safe spaces in the workplace. This is where those things can come into play. You can start by providing training for your DEI allies and managers on how to facilitate safe spaces and different perspectives in the workplace. Additionally, as we've discussed, when injustices happen, acknowledge them and create space for conversation.

This may also be the place to address resistors who keep the work from moving forward, especially if they are vocal detractors who limit the efficacy of creating psychologically safe spaces. Later in the book, you'll find a bonus step dedicated to addressing resistors.

Support employees through social justice issues.
I shared earlier that when social injustices arise, silence is not a strategy. Creating a psychologically safe space for conversation and having plans in place before injustices occur are two top ways to provide employee support. Again, I liken this to the calling in versus calling out approach. If we are proactive in handling, and not avoiding, tough situations, we create opportunities to call people into the work. This approach also helps organizations avoid being called out for lack of or a poor response.

You can empower employee resource groups with resources and flexibility to pull people together in ways they find appropriate. This might start with listening and talking circles and then move into collective actions taken by people looking for "what's next."

A good communication plan is key here, especially when it comes to acknowledging collective and social fatigue. Shift from reactive responses to proactive responses, and develop strategies that connect to your DEI vision rather than just making people feel good. Additional areas of support include discussing mental health topics, encouraging self-care, and using Employee Assistance Program (EAP) resources when appropriate.

REFLECT AND ACT

The first four steps of the DEI roadmap lay a foundation for the key assumptions of empowering our superheroes to take root. These steps help our organizations and employees understand DEI work can't wait. We're encouraged to build an internal tribe of key partners, champions, and leaders early in the process, and we want to map a clear, written DEI vision that makes executing the work possible. And we never want to keep our DEI plan a secret.

It's not that we'll do everything perfectly in all of those four steps. However, taking quality time to work through each step and to meet our benchmarks will put us in a better position to empower others. Working through the steps also helps us when dealing with the "delusional" DEI leader I mentioned before. It's easy for us to check off the boxes and say "We've done this. We've done that. But when we get here, I feel stuck." Most times when we're feeling stuck, although we hate to admit it, our feeling is a result of not having done the foundational work. A step has been skipped or skimmed. Once we have gone through each of these steps with transparency and deep work, we'll be ready to empower others to do this work.

1. **Reflect.** Consider your past and current training programs. How do you know if these programs are changing behaviors? Next, think about the systems that have been built out of policies and traditional practices. Do they support the DEI roadmap?

2. **Act.** Begin the process of reviewing your current policies and practices. Keep the following question in mind: In what ways does this policy or this practice serve as a benefit or barrier to our DEI work? This allows us to go back and add to our Roadmap the strategies we'll use to empower our employees or DEI team.

KEY TAKEAWAYS

- DEI takes more than passion. It requires upskilling, tools, and resources to be effective.

- Our learning and development should focus on changing attitudes and behaviors.

- Policies, routines, systems, and practices are either a benefit or a barrier to DEI work.

- Psychological safety is key to this DEI work.

- Silence is never a good strategy.

Step 6

PLAN DEI VICTORIES

I REMEMBER THE WORDS I used to reassure a DEI leader at a large nonprofit organization. She and her team had been working for several months with what they felt were no tangible results. Although they had a plan to follow, there was a looming gap between their current state of affairs and their desired state.

"The DEI journey is worth it," I told her. "No matter how daunting and time consuming, you can make progress, and you should celebrate your successes."

My experience has shown me that once success checkpoints are built into a roadmap, organizations see a team-wide morale boost. Where we are now, at Step 6, is all about that: planning victories, maintaining morale, and building momentum. The DEI journey is never-ending. But we're human; we need to see progress if we're to keep going. This is why it's important to proactively build in short-term wins and celebrate them.

Besides, we want meaningful results. The operative word here is *meaningful*. We can block our own efforts if we pretend we've made progress when we haven't. People, especially underrepresented groups, can see when disingenuous efforts are delivering fluff outcomes.

On the other hand, small but genuine wins can have a big impact. A *Harvard Business Review* research piece on the power of small wins calls this the *progress principle*. The progress principle states:

> Of all the things that can boost emotions, motivation, and perceptions during a workday, the single most important is making progress in meaningful work. And the more frequently people experience that sense of progress, the more likely they are to be creatively productive in the long run.[1]

We've talked quite a bit about the people part of this work. In Step 1, we discussed how to obtain the initial buy-in. In Steps 2 and 3, we talked about the importance of a governance structure that ensures someone will provide strategic leadership for the work. In Step 5, we took a deep dive on the need to equip, and empower others to join us on the journey. However, once we have the people involved, it's important for us to shift our line of thinking to how we can keep everyone actively involved over the long haul. The short answer? Demonstrate that the work is worthwhile and is making a positive difference for everyone.

I always want to emphasize a few key assumptions when it comes to demonstrating DEI victories. The first is that short-term wins provide evidence the journey is worth it and is working. We all like to know what we're doing has real results. The second assumption is that employees will support and stay motivated to accomplish DEI work if they see meaningful results early in the journey. Because DEI work is a long game, I try to weave meaningful results into the first twelve to twenty-four months of efforts—ideally, even before this. It's like a fad diet: many people quit after the first few days or weeks because they don't see instant, visible results. Setting real and realistic milestones, or strategic victories, on a timeline will help set realistic expectations for employees.

The third key assumption is that the wins must be planned and strategic. We need to be clear about how the win will be defined, when it can be expected, and what the achievement means regarding our organization's DEI progress. And the final assumption has to do with communicating our DEI strategic victories. Remember the DEI communication plan from Step 4? We already noted the primary purpose of the communication plan is to keep employees and external stakeholders informed. But we also want to strategically build real, motivating wins into the plan.

Additionally, how we communicate these successes is vitally important. Broad and consistent communication helps keep excitement levels high. I can't tell you how many times I've worked with organizations that are doing a lot of good things. In fact, they're often doing exactly the right things. But they're doing such a poor job of communicating that work and progress that people have no idea what's actually happening. In the stakeholder's mind, nothing's happening. Although this perception might not line up with reality, it becomes its own reality. So alongside building strategic victories that demonstrate results, it's essential we ensure our victories—and how we celebrate them privately and publicly—are built into the plan.

When we affirm success by creating, communicating, and celebrating small wins, we soon see other benefits as well, including:

- **Overcoming resistance.** Visible successes can sway skeptics, encouraging them to see the value in the change and to embrace it.

- **Enhancing credibility.** Demonstrating progress and substantial outcomes establishes a track
record of success. This, in turn, fosters trust and
encourages greater buy-in.

- **Mitigating risks.** Planning short-term victories
allows for better risk management. By checking
on our progress more frequently, we can identify
and address challenges, roadblocks, or potential
issues early, minimizing the overall risks associ-
ated with the change process.

- **Facilitating learning and adaptation.** Each
small victory can be assessed to understand what
worked well, what can be improved, and what
changes can be applied to future stages of the initiative. This iterative learning process allows for
continuous improvement as well as course cor-
rection as needed.

Propelling Actions

When it comes to planning DEI victories, there are specific
strategies (the "what") and real actions (the "how") that we
should incorporate into our plan. Each strategy is supported
by actions that can help everyone across the organization
understand our shared work is not in vain, nor is it superficial.
It also encourages everyone to keep pushing forward when
things get uncomfortable and progress seems far off.

Define visible DEI performance improvements.

The first strategy for planning DEI victories is to define visible DEI performance improvements. Thinking about our big
DEI goals, what results will indicate we're making progress?

Remember the desired goal is outcomes, not just outputs. Outputs are fleeting in nature. While they sometimes make people feel good, giving us a sense we're accomplishing something, the impact rarely creates real behavioral and systemic change that endures. Shifting from outputs to outcomes creates an opportunity for the measures to produce lasting, impactful results.

We started this process when we developed our strategic roadmap in Step 3. Now might be a good time to go back and revisit your strategic areas of focus, adding specific individual performance goals to the plan. For example, as a starting point, we might determine that we'll tie compensation to DEI goals for top leadership. (If this seems radical, we might ask why it feels challenging!)

You'll want to outline definitions, goals, and progress. Additionally, communicate progress on determined KPIs, outcomes, and priorities. Use the communication strategies you named in Step 4.

Recognize and affirm employees contributing to wins.

The second strategy for staging DEI victories is related to those doing the work. As DEI leaders and allies, we want to recognize and affirm employees contributing to the wins. Rewards should also be a part of their experience. There is a benefit in honoring those who are part of the work. We should do this is in culturally intelligent ways. Different people like to be acknowledged in different ways.

Recognition drives impact across multiple dimensions of a business, including employee satisfaction and retention. Yet according to a Gallup and Workhuman workplace study, 81 percent of leaders say recognition is not a major strategic priority for their organization.[2] Investment in recognition sends a powerful message to employees about what the organization values. Recognition can also shield employees from burnout, which is a critical consideration, given the nature of DEI work.

This is a good place to mention that one thing that can stall DEI progress is employee turnover. If organizations experience high employee turnover, there is likely to be a source of system-wide dissatisfaction somewhere, and it's worth determining where that is. Likewise, if the team is constantly changing, long-term DEI goals can be harder to achieve.

All of which is to say, it behooves a company to invest in the recognition of its employees. When this happens, there can be a trickle-down effect. Not only will employees who are spot-lighted for their DEI contributions be more satisfied, but those in marginalized groups will take hope in the conviction that their organization is making progress toward diversity, equity, and inclusion.

A number of other actions can help us recognize and affirm employee contributions to small wins. One best practice is highlighting contributions and stories in your employee news-letter, on your website, or on other intranet platforms. Ideally, you'll shine the spotlight on progress while simultaneously affirming the desired behaviors demonstrated by employees. I frequently recommend this strategy because it doesn't incur any additional cost to the organization, nor does it require extensive labor. Additionally, it reinforces step 4 in sharing your DEI vision.

Another simple action is to send a personal note of appre-ciation. This can come from the CDO, CEO, or other influ-ential DEI ally in the organization. This might seem obvious and elementary, but you would be amazed how many organi-zations don't take advantage of this kind and powerful gesture.

Although there is virtually no cost, it does require a small time commitment. Just like you shouldn't underestimate the influence of resistors, don't overlook the influence and impact of a kind and thoughtful note. A personal note says, "We see you and value your contribution to this work. We value you."

I helped one of my clients, a large global risk management firm, design and implement an Executive Sponsor Program for their high-potential employees of color. The program was part of their overall DEI strategy. After the initial launch, the CEO sent personal letters to each of the program participants, thanking them for being part of the program, wishing them success, and offering them access to him as they navigated the program. The participants couldn't believe it! That small act further convinced them the organization was serious about DEI, that they were valued, and that their participation in such a program was instrumental in propelling the DEI work forward.

Two other actions to consider are financial reward and promotion to a Diversity Champion to help further lead the work and role model for others. These two actions are rooted in putting your money where your mouth is and allocating dollars toward the growth of this work. It's investing directly back into the people who are investing their time and efforts in propelling it forward.

Reflect and Act

Step 6 is all about helping people see and experience progress, one small victory at a time, by integrating all these ideas and actions into a single plan. Cumulatively, these wins can have a transformative effect on your DEI efforts. They promote a positive-change culture, engage and keep stakeholders motivated, and set the stage for successful long-term change implementation.

Take some time to think through what creating, communicating, and celebrating small victories could look like for your organization. Then add your specifics to your DEI strategic roadmap.

1. **Reflect.** What small wins can you plan for the next six to twelve months? How will you celebrate and communicate those wins?

2. **Act.** Go back to your DEI Strategic Roadmap and build your small wins into the plan. Then add details to your DEI communication plan about how you will communicate and celebrate these wins.

KEY TAKEAWAYS

• Creating wins early in the journey demonstrates DEI efforts are worthwhile and working.

• Planned victories must be strategic, planned, and authentic.

• Wins motivate employees to keep doing the work.

• Employees contributing to DEI success should be recognized and affirmed.

• DEI wins must be effectively communicated across the organization.

STEP 7:
USE THE SNOWBALL EFFECT

SNOWBALL EFFECT IS when one action or event causes an expansion of outcomes, and then that expansion causes yet another. Larger and larger grows the snowball. The concept is simple. Start small, allowing each activity to grow bigger and build momentum as you work toward your goal.

We sometimes hear about this concept in relation to tackling debt. However, the snowball effect also can happen with human behavior. Think about the old philosopher's warning: *Watch your thoughts; they become words. Watch your words; they become deeds. Watch your deeds; they become habits. Watch your habits; they become character. Character is everything.* In this case, the warning is all about avoiding the negative snowball effect of our thoughts.

A similar warning should be applied to the bias snowball effect. "With the bias snowball effect," one article says, "bias is not only cascading from one stage to another, but bias increases as irrelevant information from a variety of sources is integrated and influences each other."[1] In his book *Thinking, Fast and Slow*, Nobel prize winner Daniel Kahneman breaks down how unconscious bias—the unintended, subtle, and subconscious thoughts all of us have—works, and how those thoughts have a snowball effect on our judgment and decision making. He describes two systems in our brains. System

1 is the intuitive thinking side of the brain. Our thoughts are unconscious, automatic, emotional, fast, and effortless. System 2, on the other hand, is the rational thinking side of our brain. Here, we are much more conscious, deliberate, systematic, slow, and intentional in our thinking. Most of us believe we operate on a regular basis out of System 2. The reality is that most of the time, we function in System 1.[2]

When our System 1 thinking doesn't negatively impact others, it's not a problem. But when those unconscious, automatic, fast, and effortless thoughts couple with unfair and negative assumptions about individuals or cultural groups, it becomes dangerously problematic. If we are not careful, as the old philosopher suggested, these System 1 thoughts will snowball into words, negative judgments, and decisions, eventually creating systems, policies, and practices that perpetuate inequitable experiences for others, particularly historically excluded groups.

Think back to the "Are you his scheduler?" example. I often think about the bias that was present in that woman's comment, the limited information she had, her awareness of my race and gender, and how she connected all those factors to form her own ignorant assumptions. It started in her thoughts and then turned into words. Without passing judgment on her character, it seems highly probable that her thoughts and words would influence her judgment when making decisions related to fairly hiring and promoting individuals who looked like me. It was essentially the bias snowball effect in action.

Conversely, a positive snowball effect can directly impact our approach to DEI. In Step 6, we talked about planning DEI victories. If we use these planned victories to build momentum, eventually our outcomes will be larger and more impactful than they were at the start. We need to remember it takes concentrated effort to initiate the first move and to keep it snowballing in a positive direction.

The snowball effect comes into play when several small yet significant actions begin to build upon themselves, becoming larger and growing faster. Leveraging your DEI tribe to use their credibility and momentum to create even more change beyond those small victories is both possible and critical at this stage.

So, at this point, our tribe should be extremely active in the work. And it is the job of whoever provides strategic leadership to ensure the tribe has the resources and support they need to keep things moving forward. Questions to consider here include:

- What is the next step toward change in this process?

- What do we need to change, and what are we willing to do?

- How can our tribe's credibility and momentum be used to continuously create more positive change?

A number of people start this challenging journey alone or as part of a small DEI committee or council appointed to lead these efforts. A lot of times, we have little time for DEI work because it is being shared with other important responsibilities. If this is your experience, you could probably use a break or at least some reliable help. Step 7 helps you share the work more broadly. It's the point at which you will want to take a hard look at whether or not you need to expand paid staff to support this work.

Propelling Actions

Let's get into some specific strategies around snowballing our efforts and producing change. The first strategy is to use credibility from those early wins and victories to continue changing systems, policies, practices, and routines that undermine the DEI vision. Based on these wins, leadership is typically more willing to support the DEI tribe and other superheroes, enabling them to go deeper, making more change.

A second strategy for snowballing our efforts is to keep top leadership visible in our DEI work. This helps sustain the urgency of the work. Their participation signals to others within the organization that this work is real and necessary and that we are committed to it.

Third, we can gain much by having a strategy for hiring, promoting, and developing employees who are eager to help implement the DEI vision. If this work is really important to our organization, we will demonstrate our commitment by allocating the necessary resources—both human and financial. Just as important, we want to compensate and position the person who is leading the work to have decision-making power to create real impact and lasting systems change.

Whenever I'm asked to visit and consult with organizations who have hired someone to lead their DEI work, I ask two questions. First, to whom does the person responsible for the DEI work report? And second, what is their budget? The answers tell me almost everything I need to know about the top leadership's level of commitment to the work. Ideally, the DEI staffperson should be in a senior leadership role and have a straight line to the CEO. And their budget should be more than a line item for a few training programs throughout the year.

If you want to snowball your efforts, compensate your DEI leaders fairly and competitively. Furthermore, set them up for success by positioning them as genuine leaders and giving them the resources they need to succeed.

A final strategy connects to snowballing enthusiasm. DEI work is exhausting, in part because it is never ending. This is why I place such a strong emphasis on having a plan for our own mental health while carrying the weight of this work. It's hugely helpful if we can keep people excited about the work. A significant part of your snowballing efforts is in your ability to reinvigorate the change process with new projects and DEI champions. Enthusiasm and fresh perspectives are needed to combat the inevitable exhaustion and to accommodate the long and arduous process of DEI change.

Let's move into what operationalizing these strategies might look like.

Use credibility from early wins.

Using credibility from early wins is the first strategy for snowballing DEI efforts. Not only do you want to communicate the wins, as determined in Step 6, but you also want to leverage those wins to shout from the mountain top, "We're making progress!" This is the snowballing part of it. Armed with evidence of real progress, leaders are usually more open to taking a more thoughtful look at other systems, policies, and practices that may need to be changed. In practice, using the credibility of wins can look like one of these actions:

- **Make a big deal of wins, and communicate them using every available vehicle.** The wins, no matter how small, are a big deal. From newsletters to internal memos, from the company Slack channel to other available media, progress should be shared. We don't want to sit on our wins by waiting too long to share them. While there may be a formal process for getting news like this into the company newsletter, it's a great idea to let employees know in real time that they're doing a good job. Letting them know a specific action has been helpful or progressive in the moment reinforces desired behaviors or actions.

- **Regularly assess what is or isn't working to decide what needs to be improved.** Not everything our DEI tribe and others implement will work, and that's normal and okay. But it is important to regularly assess what is or isn't working and what contributing factors produce the results we see. We need to take time to evaluate systems and processes without fear of the truth or failure. If we learn from our mistakes and pivot when necessary, we can move forward confidently. We need quality data to support our decisions. Additionally, look for adequate time for real assessment before changing rapidly. Some strategies require more time than others to be recognized, planned, or implemented.

- **Celebrate the accomplishment of goals.** I can honestly say I've missed moments to celebrate my own achievements because I was so focused on the next thing. That said, I also realize that pausing to celebrate accomplishments fuels my desire to achieve more. Make time to celebrate goal achievement with your teams. It's another way to keep the momentum of and excitement around your efforts moving forward.

Keep leadership visible.

Leadership is more important than ever at this stage. Keeping your organization's leaders visible in the work helps sustain the urgency you created at the beginning. This can look like leadership continuing to host and support town hall meetings. Your organization may call them listening sessions or inclusion circles. Whatever language you use, it's paramount that leadership stays in front of people, continues to listen, and accepts feedback from stakeholders both within and outside the organization.

The presence of leadership should demonstrate that an organization's senior people are just as committed to the work six to twelve months down the line as they were at the onset. This may look like an annual transparency report that includes a personal statement on diversity. Leadership can say, "It's December 31. These are the wins we've had. Here are the outcomes of the efforts and results of the assessments. Here's where we need to grow."

The transparency report is designed to be just that: transparent. The use of these kinds of reports indicates leaders' acknowledgment of the importance of accountability and that there's still opportunity and commitment to improve. This acknowledgment is good; it's part of the process. All these efforts are about keeping the urgency of the work in front of people and ensuring that leadership is a core part of the DEI experience.

Hire others to implement the DEI vision.

I mentioned earlier that Step 7 is the one where additional resources and support are often needed. Specifically, this step on the roadmap is where the efforts and resulting outcomes have built a solid case for needing more paid resources on the team. In addition to supporting the CDO, the most effective organizations are those that can honestly evaluate staffing needs, and be open to expanding the people on the CDO's team. It could be a DEI manager, a DEI learning and development manager, a DEI program designer, or whatever titles you might use at your organization.

As you have gained momentum, you will also have experienced some positive results and feel ready to expand the work. This is the moment reality starts setting in. It's the moment leadership and the DEI tribe begin to think, "Clearly, we are going to need more staff to help us do this. We can't just rely on allies volunteering to do the work." In addition to using their influence to impact change, leaders' support for more DEI team personnel can be urgent.

Reinvigorate with new projects and DEI allies.

A final action for snowballing your efforts is reinvigorating your projects and people. This can be done through at least three specific actions:

1. **Develop a system and process that creates an ongoing pipeline of diversity allies.** I cannot overemphasize how challenging and draining DEI work can be, especially when nearly all the efforts rest on one person. I'm a firm believer in

the old adage: "Many hands make for light work." Because DEI is such a necessary part of organizational success, it's important to give attention to how we create an ongoing pipeline of diversity allies.

I like to start by defining leadership competencies and identifying potential talent that may exhibit these competencies. Executive coach Meredith Moore suggests creating an ongoing pipeline of diversity to "openly share your commitment to diversity and development."[3] Think back to equipping superheroes in this work. When others know they will be supported as they grow in this work, they'll be more likely to come forward.

We already know most individuals coming to the table are not DEI experts. Even so, some can be identified as potential successors for eventual DEI leadership roles. Developing a formal mentor and sponsorship program for these individuals can be extremely effective in preparing them for success in these new roles.

2. **Facilitate ongoing training and development with DEI allies.** Remember, DEI allies are not experts. Upskilling them is important. Their ongoing training can happen in a variety of ways—continuing education programs, peer learning and networking, and coaching are just a few ideas.

This is also an opportunity to look at the organization's investment in DEI. Are there webinars, resources, or case studies that others can leverage to stay updated on best practices? If not, a very modest investment to procure these resources can pay high returns.

Remember that ongoing training should be complemented by a supportive and safe organizational culture that values and prioritizes DEI efforts. We try to avoid requiring folks to participate in professional development just to check a box. Remember, the goal is skill building, behavior change, and sustainable practice, not performative lists. However we facilitate the development of the team, we should also regularly assess the impact of training programs, and adjust such programs based on feedback and evolving needs.

3. **Use employee feedback to inform new ideas, strategies, and projects.** Leadership mentor Michael Hyatt and his daughter Megan Hyatt Miller have shared how soliciting feedback from employees is key to growth for leaders. According to Hyatt, feedback "is free, doesn't cost us anything, and it's readily available, people would love the opportunity to talk about your leadership, but they need permission and they need to know that it's a safe environment to do so."[4]

I believe the same holds true when we are talking about DEI progress. Employees need a safe space to share what's working, what's not, and to contribute to what happens next. This can be facilitated through anonymous surveys, employee resource groups, focus groups, listening sessions, or other collaborative and transparent communication methods that will lead to fresh ideas.

Whatever route we take, the key to success is to actually take action on the feedback provided. We need to share updates on how previous feedback has informed specific initiatives or projects, showcasing the impact and the progress made. By leveraging employee feedback effectively, we can harness the collective intelligence and perspectives of our workforce, leading to more inclusive and impactful DEI strategies and projects.

Despite the seriousness of DEI work, it doesn't have to be stale. By reinvigorating projects and keeping a pipeline of well-equipped allies alive and well, we set up our organizations for success. We only need to remember that DEI work is everyone's responsibility and that momentum grows the snowball of success.

REFLECT AND ACT

Leverage planned victories and early efforts to drive impact and outcomes into a snowball effect. Take time here to give real attention to what this can look like in practice for your own team or organization.

1. **Reflect.** Are you already snowballing your DEI efforts? If so, how? Do you have the right team in place to take your DEI efforts to the next level?

2. **Act.** Identify specific strategies for snowballing your efforts. Go back and build them into your roadmap. If necessary, adjust your DEI budget and take the leap to expand your DEI team with more paid staff.

KEY TAKEAWAYS

• Building momentum and creating more behavioral and system change is critical to keeping people engaged in the work.

• Expanding your DEI tribe with more paid staff will demonstrate the organization's ongoing commitment and will create greater impact and results.

• Keeping top leadership front and center is critical.

• Developing a pipeline of DEI allies and leaders helps to sustain the work.

PHASE 3
MAKING IT LAST

Step 8

MAKE DEI LAST

RECENTLY, A FORMER client reached out to me, wanting to re-engage in some DEI work. He was the top leader of his organization, and it had been a few years since we had worked together. As he shared his needs, it all began to sound very familiar. In fact, I said to him, "This looks like the same work we did three years ago. We spent several months assessing your organization's state as it relates to DEI and spending time upskilling staff leadership and the board. I think we agreed on several specific recommendations to move the work forward. Why do you imagine you're in the same spot three years later?"

As a consultant in this work for over a quarter of a century, I've learned I can describe for my clients what they need to do, but I can't make them do it. And this scenario reminded me, once again, that if organizations don't fully commit to all the steps in this change process, and if top leadership doesn't keep their foot on the gas pedal, the work will quickly get sidetracked or bogged down. Change doesn't last without reinforcement.

At this point in the journey, we've assessed where our organization is on the DEI journey, and we've created a roadmap to propel the work forward. We're building momentum and seeing positive results. But how do we make these changes last? How do we make the work stick? We want to confidently know and say, "DEI is part of the DNA of our organization. It is who we are as an organization. It's a feature of our organizational character." But this requires a culture change that's thorough and persistent. We all know how hard it is and how long it takes to change an organization's culture.

Organizational culture is the shared ideas, customs, assumptions, expectations, philosophy, traditions, and values that determine how a group of people will behave.[1] Another way to put this is that organizational culture is "the way we do things around here."

Effective change builds on an existing culture. If people don't understand the why, what, and how of the change, they will resist it. (We'll talk more about this in the next bonus step on dealing with resistors.) Even when people embrace the change, the process to create that culture change is long and intense. This is why top leadership has to stay in the forefront of the work. Their contribution is not optional.

The final stage in this change process will walk us through specific strategies that will create staying power for embedding DEI into our organizational identity and culture. It's about making DEI last. And while I'd love to tell you this is the final phase, the truth is we'll always need to keep cycling through the three phases. By this point, your DEI roadmap should be good, but it's like the maps and GPS apps we use. They require regular updates.

Similar to the other steps in this process, we should consider a few assumptions here in Step 8. The first is that new efforts tend to last in the culture when it's clear they are producing results. This goes beyond the sometimes false assumption that because we are busy with DEI activities, things are improving. As we discussed earlier, you can probably think of a time or two when there was a disconnect in your organization between the executive leadership's expectations and the rest of the organization's experience or perception. Sometimes, it's a communication issue. Other times, it's because the efforts (or lack of them) have simply not been effective. This is the type of disconnect we're correcting when we're working to make DEI last. Not only do the efforts actually have to be taking place, but they also must be communicated effectively and consistently, showing a bottom-line impact. It may be helpful to think back to Step 4, where we created a plan for communicating the vision and roadmap; or Step 6, with its planned victories; or also Step 7, where we snowballed our efforts.

A second assumption surrounds new practices and sustainability. Our DEI roadmap needs to lead to long-lasting change, and that includes promotion and succession planning. However, if our promotion and succession processes are incompatible with our new practices, the old culture will force its way back in place. In other words, as we develop a pipeline of DEI leaders and allies, their competencies and skills must continually match the required tasks.

Let's say part of our DEI strategy includes the formation or expansion of employee resource groups (ERGs). These are usually voluntary, employee-led groups intended to foster an inclusive work environment for cultural groups that have been historically excluded. ERGs can be a very effective strategy. However, Robert Rodriguez, author of *Employee Resource Group Excellence*, argues that very often these groups end up being known as the "food, flags, and fun" groups. That's because they tend to default to social events and activities.[2]

This is, at least in part, because the individuals leading these groups lack the experience and skills to be effective. They are often left on their own to develop an ERG strategy that will increase employee engagement. In addition, while the allies they manage are often passionate about the work, they are also often volunteers who have no direct reporting relationship to the ERG leaders. Plus, they usually have little to no budget.

Again, without proper upskilling and resources—including compensation—this type of promotion and succession strategy doesn't align with the broader commitment, goals, and practices that are part of the DEI roadmap. Ultimately, this will undermine the ability of the work to last.

The scenario I shared at the beginning of this chapter and the ERG case are clear examples of how we can easily and quickly derail our own efforts. On the other hand, we can often learn from best practices that will enable all of our work to last.

Propelling Actions

When it comes to making DEI work last, there are two critical strategies, and they involve communication and succession planning. It's imperative to effectively demonstrate the relationship between these two and how they, combined, can create lasting change. Let's look into ways to incorporate both of these into the DNA of the organization.

Communicate connections and transformation.

The first key to making DEI stick is to clearly and consistently communicate the relationship between the new behaviors and systems and the success the organization is experiencing. Everyone needs to understand, for example, that both the unconscious bias training and the managers' cultural intelligence training has had a direct impact on the diversity of the talent pool and behavior change. If we aren't communicating this, that's a big miss. If, as another example, we aren't able to help folks connect the dots between our policy change on accessibility and how employees from the neurodivergent community have increased their level of engagement, that's another miss. Or, as yet another example, if they don't see how the launch of an executive sponsorship program helped to retain and promote X number of people of color into top leadership roles in the organization, your efforts to make DEI last will be compromised.

Clearly demonstrate the before and after within the organization. Who doesn't love a good before and after? There are entire shows, from home improvement to personal appearance, built on creating major transformations. DEI is no different. We must be able to show and tell the "now and then" story of how things used to be and the transformation that has happened. Furthermore, there needs to be clear communication surrounding the efforts it takes to maintain the transformation.

The change we want is sustainable. When communicating the transformation, it is not enough to just state it once or twice. We need to continue presenting results (before versus after) on a regular basis. We also want to use reporting to show how the transformation benefits employees and the organization. We need to make this kind of communication part of our DEI communication plan. It's what enables us to develop DEI goals for leaders and, eventually, all employees.

Create leadership development and succession plans.

Another strategy for making DEI work last is to create leadership development and succession plans consistent with the DEI strategic roadmap. Everyone across the organization should be on a learning journey, including top leadership. At this stage, continue including DEI goals, learning and development, and action plans in leadership development plans. Set clear expectations for inclusive leadership and behavior, and hold everyone accountable.

Part of this process should also include actively working toward increased diverse representation in top leadership roles, ensuring that the organization's pattern of diversity reflects the diverse patterns of its customers and stakeholders. It can also include removing or restructuring resistors, if necessary. And of course, you'll want to revisit and adjust the strategic roadmap as necessary and conduct an annual assessment to ensure you're staying on track and moving things forward.

Integrate DEI into long-term strategic planning processes.

We spoke earlier about the importance of DEI being an integral part of the overall business strategy. It should also be built into the long-term strategic planning processes. Goals and strategies should seamlessly fit into the organization's strategic plan, annual objectives, and operational activities. And as mentioned earlier, each department should have a DEI strategy for their area. What, for example, does DEI look like in the admissions department or IT?

This is also a good occasion to again revisit how DEI connects to efforts related to corporate social responsibility and environmental, social, and governance investing. The combination influences culture change with long-term sustainability and has a convincing impact on the bottom line.

Conduct an annual or biyearly DEI assessment.

As part of our effort to make the work last, it's wise to conduct an annual DEI assessment. This is another way to stay on top of how employees are perceiving our DEI efforts and where we may be missing the boat. The feedback can be used to update, and make changes to our roadmap.

In addition to the annual assessment, you can facilitate quarterly pulse surveys throughout the year to see what, if any, adjustments need to be made. These can help us catch challenges or opportunities for change before they become big issues and curtail our work. We can, with wise input, course correct faster, rather than waiting for the end-of-year survey results.

As we wrap up this section, I want to note that there's a bonus step that follows this one, on dealing with resistors. However, I want to pause here and preface that step by reminding you that this is the stage of the process where we must have deeper, more serious conversations about how resistors align (or not) within the organization's DEI culture and goals. You may discover that some individuals who are not willing to come on board with DEI work may not be the best employee for the organization and where it is going. And they may need to transition out. That's okay.

Making DEI work last is not easy and, like the other steps, major cultural change doesn't happen overnight. But paying attention to and implementing the strategies outlined here are critical to embedding DEI into the fiber of your organization and creating enduring transformational change.

Reflect and Act

Making DEI work stick takes effort in both communication and consistency. A level of accountability is also required. Consider how you will incorporate these realities into your roadmap.

1. **Reflect.** What strategies will you use to make DEI endure in your organization?

2. **Act.** Identify strategies to make DEI sustainable within your organization. Determine how you will measure success and build in accountability. Go back and adjust your DEI strategic roadmap accordingly.

KEY TAKEAWAYS

- DEI efforts will last in the culture when it's clear they produce results.

- We must clearly and consistently communicate the relationship between new behaviors and systems and the successes the organization is experiencing.

- Our DEI roadmap needs to be integrated into our overall business strategy and connect to existing efforts.

- If promotion and succession planning are not aligned with our new practices, the old culture will force its way back in place.

Bonus Step

HANDLING RESISTORS

SEVERAL TIMES IN the early steps, I mentioned resistors. You may even have a specific person in mind when you hear that. But before we unpack the *how* of working with resistors, let's consider *why* people resist our efforts.

Researchers who study the psychological roots of resisting change discuss three of the most common forms of resistance, especially within DEI work. They are status threat, merit threat, and moral threat.[1] These threats and concerns often come from the dominant culture in an organization who have historically benefitted from being in the majority and feel their status or resources are in jeopardy if they embrace DEI. This is the *status threat*, and those who experience it often view DEI as a zero-sum game: If you win, I lose. The assumption is that if a member of the underrepresented population makes any gains through hiring or promotion, or even recognition, those in the majority will suffer a loss.

Another psychological challenge is *merit threat.* This is when some team members fear that DEI initiatives imply their achievements are not the result of their skills and qualities but rather their cultural group membership. A few years ago, I wrote an article called "Fact or Myth: We Can't Find Diverse Candidates for Our Team."[2] I noted there that if I were paid a dollar for every time I heard someone say, "We just can't find qualified people to diversify our team" or "We just want to hire the best-qualified candidate," I could have retired and moved to paradise years ago. More importantly, I argued that the notion that it's impossible or difficult to find high-quality diverse job candidates, particularly those from underrepresented groups, needs to be dismantled.

Individuals who struggle with merit threat are often part of an advantaged group and feel that recognizing the existence of bias, discrimination, and inequities somehow minimizes or explains away their own success. Merit threat is especially common in organizations that tout high performance and individual merit as high organizational values. The challenge comes when there is a bias and assumption that diversity automatically means a compromise in competence and performance.

I was facilitating a DEI strategic planning session with a team of C-suite leaders in an industry that is predominately full of white males when this topic came up. Several of the leaders said repeatedly, "We want diversity, but our priority is hiring the best high-performing candidate for the job." My response was, "Why do you feel the two—diversity and high performance—are in conflict?" I went on to say, "If you truly value diversity, why are you still a visibly predominately white organization?"

Some would argue, "We are diverse! For example, there's diversity of thought." This is a form of diversity, yes, and important to include in the conversation. But it's often and easily used as a scapegoat and argument for not addressing a lack of visible diversity. These questions opened the door to some honest, even courageous dialogue about our real level of commitment to DEI. Out of that dialogue, we began to gain some real traction.

Finally, researchers argue that those in the dominant culture can sometimes experience *moral threat*. This is the notion that if you acknowledge your privilege, power, and biases, you tarnish your moral reputation by linking yourself to the DEI cause. This is common when individuals, including DEI allies, are generally committed to the moral ideal of DEI. Because people want to be perceived as morally good, they may experience threat when a DEI initiative exposes how their cultural group, and the systems that support the traditional culture, or even their own actions, have violated a moral principle.

When these three threats are experienced, the response is typically one of three types of resistance, or a combination of all three: 1) defending the status quo, 2) denying the inequities, or 3) distancing themselves from the situation. Understanding the root causes of resistance to change and analyzing which ones are prevalent in our organization are prerequisites to the process of obtaining buy-in. Once you have that consent, especially from leaders, there are effective and proven strategies for getting people on board with the work.

PROPELLING ACTIONS

Identify and address resistors.
Just as we want to identify our allies quickly, we want to identify and address our resistors as rapidly as possible. With this being an anticipated 25 percent of the organization, it's important to take the time to understand why they resist. We may find that a resistor's reasoning is something that we can work with, help resolve, or move toward supporting. This may be as simple as one-on-one meetings or surveys.

Although resistors are a minority percentage of the organization and we want to spend most of our time on believers and allies, we don't want to completely underestimate their power. Instead, we want to leverage our allies to engage them. For example, if you know you have a resistor who's over in Department A and they're not listening to you, but you see the resistor respects Mike, who's over Department B and is totally on board with the DEI plan, you might leverage Mike to work with the resistor over in Department A. Let Mike talk with that person, peer to peer, about why this work is important. Get the resistor involved. Use storytelling as a strategy. Demonstrate the business case. Listen to their concerns. But while doing the necessary work with resistors, spend most of your energy on your believers and allies. The resistors matter, but they don't matter most.

Stay focused where it matters.

Take that initial step to understand who your resistors are, and then take a second step to understand why they might be resisting. If there's a way to close the gap and bring them on board by using things like storytelling and leveraging your allies, do that. But beyond that, if they continue to resist, do not allow them to drain all your energy and time. Focus on those individuals who are with you and want to be equipped to support the implementation of the work.

REFLECT AND ACT

At the beginning of this book, when I first mentioned resistors, I'm sure a person or two popped into your mind. You've also probably been thinking about their negativity and how to "fix" it as you've worked through the steps in this book. As part of that process, I invite you to reflect and act on the questions below.

1. **Reflect.** Based on what we've discussed so far, what new strategies might you use to address the resistors in your organization?

2. **Act.** Go back to your DEI strategic roadmap and add information on how the resistors will be addressed.

KEY TAKEAWAYS

- Three types of perceived threats can contribute to resistance: status threat, merit threat, and moral threat.

- Understanding the root causes of resistance to change and analyzing which ones are prevalent in our organizations are prerequisites to obtaining buy-in.

- There are proven strategies for positively addressing resistors and their threat perception to move DEI work forward. Resistors matter, but they don't matter most.

Conclusion

YOUR DEI ROADMAP

T THE END of the day it's worth repeating, DEI is all about change management: changing individual behaviors and changing systems. Neither is easy. Each is necessary. Both are possible.

You may remember that we began this book with the acknowledgment that most major change efforts fail. DEI work is no exception. DEI progress in most settings has been slow and limited. Even with some of the really good work that has been done, not enough of it has been sustained. It's not lasting.

But we don't need to be discouraged. In fact, just the opposite. When we couple our commitment to this work with a clear, evidenced-based framework and the necessary resources, real transformation can happen. The culture of an organization can change. We all can win.

To make DEI work an effective, sustained component of an organization's culture, each phase of the change management process for DEI is essential and builds upon the previous one. Let's quickly recap some of the important points in this process.

Whether you are the full-time DEI leader or have inherited a role as part of other responsibilities, your mental health on this journey matters. This is especially important for people of color and other individuals who are part of marginalized and historically excluded groups. The ugly history behind our current realities and our daily lived experiences adds another layer of stress and trauma not experienced by those in the majority culture. But everyone involved in leading this work should have a strategy in place to avoid diversity and compassion fatigue.

The first layer of mental health protection is the recognition that DEI is everyone's responsibility. Everyone in the organization is responsible for the overall progress, success, and even failure of DEI initiatives. This work is not ours alone.

The second layer of protection from burnout is determining what things we will do to avoid catastrophe when—not if—frustrations, disappointments, setbacks, and resistance arise. Start with the sense that this is very, very difficult work and that its importance does not rely on us alone. Once we're equipped with a strategy for our own personal mental health, we'll have a foundational understanding from which to work. This foundation will put us in the best position not only to start the effort but to see it through to an eventual, successful conclusion.

After developing our personal care plan and an initial, realistic assessment of our organization's current state, three phases follow eight specific steps. Two considerations should guide our caution as we move through each step:

1. We will be tempted to skim or skip steps. Don't. Each step and phase builds on the last. We must not yield to this temptation.

2. There will be resistors and critics along the way. We do not want to underestimate their power and influence, and we do not want to overestimate them either. We want to make a realistic

appraisal of them and their potential influence. Then we move forward.

The eight steps of the DEI Propel Framework move from identifying the need for immediate action to embedding our efforts into the organization's cultural DNA. Asking and answering the right and specific questions will provide a clear picture of where our organization needs to focus its efforts. Again, none of these steps should be skipped.

DEI Propel™ Framework

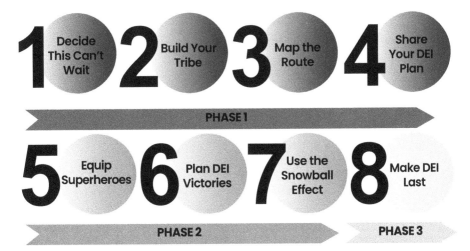

Specific strategies and actions contribute to building and executing your DEI roadmap for each step. Many of the strategies and how to operationalize them can be adapted in some way to meet your unique organizational and/or team needs.

OLD AND NEW CHALLENGES

DEI is not a destination; it's a continuous journey. Not only will we experience resistance internally; we'll also experience it externally. From the polarization of the topic to the aggressive enforcement of laws and policies that prohibit the work, we've been here before.

In *Caste: The Origins of Our Discontent,* author Isabel Wilkerson masterfully describes how America today and throughout its history has been shaped by a hidden caste system. She details how these destructive forces and systems have created and sustained divisiveness, lack of inclusion, and inequitable treatment of certain individuals and groups. She also reminds us that this isn't just an American problem. She shows in agonizing detail how the Nazis studied the racial systems in America to plan their outcast of the Jews and others and how the long-standing caste system in India is linked to systems in the United States.

Former Sodexo global chief diversity officer Rohini Anand notes, "Every place has its history of exclusion, its discrimination, its web of attitudes and systems that fuel and justify marginalization."[1] The role of global DEI practitioners is to uncover those legacies of power imbalance and to determine the strategies that will be most effective in addressing them. Again, we've been here before. We should not be surprised by current and future forms of resistance. It's often history repeating itself. Our response needs to be assertive; we must not stop fighting. One piece of powerful ammunition is our unwavering commitment to the work and a strategy that is agile and able to withstand challenges and even attacks.

For nearly three decades, I have witnessed the push and pull of DEI work. It's a tug-of-war that can leave even top practitioners weary. The DEI Propel Framework is rooted in data-driven care. Questions, easy and difficult, lead to answers that become the data driving the case for change that lasts. As we close, we can look back and ask ourselves these questions:

1. Has our initial assessment of our organizational state changed?

2. Does our DEI strategic roadmap feel realistic and doable?

3. What challenges do we anticipate as we continue with our DEI efforts? How do we plan to resolve those challenges?

The real work of implementation begins now. The good news is that we have a plan. By calling in versus calling out, we invite others on the journey. At any given point, we may need to pause and revisit the phases and steps. As we implement the work, we'll continue using data, we'll log our wins and failures, and we'll be informed by regular feedback from employees so we learn what's working and what isn't. We'll adjust accordingly.

Best success to you on your journey as you move confidently and boldly into this special work!

Resources

THIS COMPILATION OF resources, including the reading list, is a inexhaustive introduction to the background and content of this work. You might use these resources as a starting point or as a checkpoint for your continued efforts on the DEI journey. Included are the following resources:

- Reading List
- DEI Acronym Glossary
- Common DEI Definitions
- Common DEI Roles
- DEI Propel Framework
- DEI Propel Strategic Roadmap Template

Reading List

Deming, W. Edward. *Out of the Crisis.* First MIT Press edition. Cambridge, MA: MIT Press, 2000.

DiAngelo, Robin. *White Fragility: Why It's So Hard for White People to Talk About Racism.* Boston: Beacon Press, 2018.

Kendi, Ibram X. *Stamped From the Beginning : The Definitive History of Racist Ideas in America.* New York: Nation Books, 2017.

Kim, Michelle MiJung. *The Wake Up: Closing the Gap Between Good Intentions and Real Change.* New York: Hachette Go, 2021.

Kotter, John. *Leading Change.* Boston: Harvard Business Review Press, 2012.

Kotter, John P. and Dan S. Cohen. *The Heart of Change: Real-Life Stories of How People Change Their Organizations.* 1st ed. Boston: Harvard Business Review Press, 2012, 1.

Lawson, Emily and Colin Price, "*The Psychology of Change Management,*" The McKinsey Quarterly<ital>, June 1, 2003, https://www.mckinsey.com/business-functions/organization/our-insights/the-psychology-of-change-management.

Leiba, Elizabeth. *I'm Not Yelling: A Black Woman's Guide to Navigating the Workplace.* Coral Gables, FL: Mango, 2022.

Livermore, David. *Leading With Cultural Intelligence: The Real Secret to Success.* 2nd ed. New York: AMACOM, 2015.

Mattingly, Victoria, Sertrice Grice, and Allison Goldstein. *Inclusalytics: How Diversity, Equity, and Inclusion Leaders Use Data to Drive Their Work.* Independently published, 2022.

Menakem, Resmaa. My Grandmother's Hands: Racialized Trauma and the Pathway to Mending Our Hearts and Bodies. Las Vegas: Central Recovery Press, 2017.

Thomas, R. Roosevelt Jr. *World Class Diversity Management: A Strategic Approach.* Oakland, CA: Berrett-Koehler, 2010.

Wilkerson, Isabel. *Caste: The Origins of Our Discontents.* New York: Random House, 2020.

Winters, Mary-Frances. *We Can't Talk about That at Work! How to Talk about Race, Religion, Politics, and Other Polarizing Topics.* Oakland, CA: Berrett-Koehler, 2017.

DEI ACRONYM GLOSSARY

AAPI: Asian American Pacific Islander

BIPOC: Black, Indigenous, and People of Color

BLM: Black Lives Matter

BME: Black and Minority Ethnic

BRG: Business Resource Group

DEI: Diversity, Equity and Inclusion

DEIB: Diversity, Equity, Inclusion, and Belonging

DEIBA: Diversity, Equity, Inclusion, Belonging, and Accessibility

DEIJ: Diversity, Equity, Inclusion, and Justice

EAP: Employee Assistance Program

EDI: Equality, Diversity, and Inclusion

ERG: Employee Resource Group

HRBP: Human Resource Business Partners

IDEA: Inclusion, Diversity, Equity, and Accessibility

KPI: Key Performance Indicators

LGBTQI+: Lesbian, Gay, Bisexual, Transgender, Queer, Intersex, plus (+) all other identities

ORG: Objectives, Results, and Goals

POC: People of Color

PWD: People With Disabilities

Common Definitions

Ally: A person of one social identity group who stands up in support of members of another social group and who is willing to act to help end discrimination, amplify unheard voices, and protect the rights of everyone

Accessibility: The practice of making information, activities, and/or environments sensible, meaningful, and usable for as many people as possible

Belonging: The feeling of security and support when there is a sense of acceptance, inclusion and identity

Bystander: Someone who witnesses something taking place but does not participate or assume an active role positively or negatively

Change management: A set of strategies and processes used to manage organizational change and guide people through the necessary transition to achieve a desired outcome

Covering: The intentional downplaying/minimizing of a stigmatized identity in order to avoid negative perceptions or consequences

Cultural intelligence: The capability to function and relate effectively in any multicultural context

Culture: The accepted and familiar behaviors, beliefs, and assumptions about what is "normal" for members of a particular group

DEI: Any organizational effort to increase diverse representation and create inclusive, equitable environments

Disability: Functional limitations that affect one or more of the major life activities, including walking, lifting, learning and breathing

Diversity: Working to increase the representation of difference at every level of the organization

Employee resource groups (sometimes called other names): Employee-led groups whose aim is to foster an inclusive workplace

Equity: Actively challenging and responding to individual and systemic biases, behaviors, policies, and practices to ensure that every employee has fair access to opportunities

Gaslighting: Manipulating someone by psychological means into questioning their own reasonability or even sanity

Inclusion: Fostering an environment where people with different identities experience feeling welcomed, valued, and a sense of belonging

Inclusive leadership: Leaders who commit to ensuring all team members are treated equitably, feel a sense of belonging and value, and have the resources and support they need to achieve their full potential

Intersectionality: Originated by feminist theorist Kimberlé Crenshaw, the complex interaction between different stigmatized identities, such as race, class, and gender; these diversity dimensions often overlap

Key performance indicators: A set of quantifiable measures used to evaluate the performance or success of an organization's efforts

Mentor: Someone who advises you on your current role and what you need to do in order to progress through your career

Microaggressions: Everyday, subtle, and insensitive acts or behaviors that devalue others

Neurodiversity: The viewpoint that conditions like ADHD, autism, and dyslexia aren't deficits; they're simply normal variations of the human brain

Performative: Actions that are insincere or ineffective when engaging in the DEI work

Psychological safety: The belief that one will not be punished or humiliated for speaking up with ideas, questions, concerns, or mistakes

Targeted universalism: Setting universal goals pursued by targeting processes to achieve those goals

Unconscious bias: Unintended, subtle, and subconscious thoughts that happen to all of us, all of the time

COMMON DEI ROLES

Chief Diversity Officer: Develops and oversees the DEI strategy and overall diversity and inclusion efforts of an organization

Director or Manager of Diversity: Develops, implements, and monitors the organization's DEI goals and programs; creates and leads learning and development programs that foster an inclusive work environment; also builds relationships with internal and external stakeholders

Diversity and Inclusion Program Manager: Develops, implements, and monitors diversity goals and programs in various departments; creates and leads training sessions to foster an open and inclusive environment for everyone; also builds relationships with internal and external stakeholders

Diversity Business Partner: Collaborates with leaders and teams within an organization to identify best practices for diversity and inclusion; distributes diversity resources across organizations and inspires teamwork and collaboration across various organizational groups; also assists CDO and senior-level management with the development of innovative and measurable solutions to create a more DEI workplace

Diversity Recruiter: Primary role is to attract and retain a diverse workforce; may also support creating company policies that promote equality and diversity; could also facilitate training sessions for human resources managers to promote diverse hiring decisions; helps to establish fair HR and DEI policies, creates job descriptions with inclusive language, and networks with potential candidates from underrepresented groups

Diversity Trainer: Facilitates or coordinates DEI learning and development programming based on data-driven research and employee needs; also empowers and equips managers and ERG leaders and provides best practices to help create a DEI organization

Sponsor: Someone with power who recognizes your potential and actively advocates for your success on the corporate or organizational ladder

Supplier Diversity Manager: Creates a diverse supply chain network and system for the organization; develops strategies to ensure a diverse supplier base; also researches and records potential businesses owned by diverse groups or individuals for future purchases and contracts

DEI Propel™ Framework
Summary of Phases, Steps and Actions

Phase 1: Unfreezing the Current State	
Step 1: Decide This Can't Wait	**Help** your organization understand the importance and urgency of DEI to obtain buy-in.
Step 2: Build Your Tribe	**Organize** a team of DEI leaders and allies to lead the work.
Step 3: Map the Route	**Develop** a DEI vision and data-driven strategic roadmap.
Step 4: Share Your DEI Plan	**Communicate** the DEI vision and strategy constantly and consistently.
Phase Two: Introducing New DEI Practices	
Step 5: Equip Superheroes	**Educate** and **upskill** DEI allies, managers, and others so the work is shared.
Step 6: Plan DEI Victories	**Plan and celebrate** progress and short-term wins.
Step 7: Use the Snowball Effect	**Use** progress and success to create more success and organizational change.
Phase 3: Making It Last	
Step 8: Make DEI Last	**Demonstrate** the relationship between changing behaviors and systems, leadership commitment, and improved organizational culture.

DEI Propel™ Strategic Roadmap Template

Organization:
DEI Vision Statement:

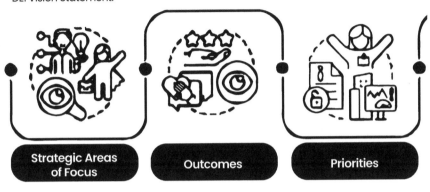

Strategic Areas of Focus **Outcomes** **Priorities**

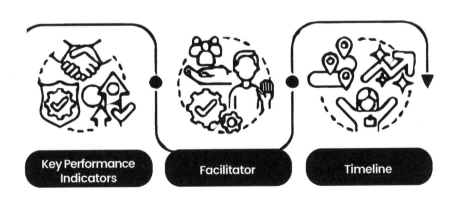

Key Performance Indicators **Facilitator** **Timeline**

Notes

PREFACE

1. Robert H. Schaffer, "All Management Is Change Management," *Harvard Business* Review, October 26, 2017, https://hbr.org/2017/10/all-management-is-change-management.

2. J. P. Kotter, *Leading Change* (Boston: Harvard Business School Press, 1996).

INTRODUCTION

1. Todd Corley, Vontrese Pamphile, and Katina Sawyer, "What Has (and Hasn't) Changed About Being a Chief Diversity Officer," *Harvard Business Review*, September 23, 2022, https://hbr.org/2022/09/what-has-and-hasnt-changed-about-being-a-chief-diversity-officer.

2. HR.com, "The Future of Diversity, Equity, and Inclusion 2022: Incorporate New DEI Initiatives to Foster Strong Employee Relationships and Increase Organizational Success," October 2022, https://www.hr.com/en/resources/free_research_white_papers/the-future-of-diversity-equity-and-inclusion-resea_l0wk79fe.html.

3. Josh Bersin and Kathi Enderes, "Elevating Equity: The Real Story of Diversity and Inclusion," 2021, https://joshbersin.com/wp-content/uploads/2021/04/202102-DEI-Report_Final_V2.pdf?utm_medium=email&_

hsmi=122877344&utm_content=122877344&utm_
source=hs_automation, 8.

4. Integrating Women Leaders Foundation, "State of Allyship-in-Action Benchmark Study," 2022, https:// iwlfoundation.org/wp-content/uploads/2023/03/ IWL-SOAIA-Report.pdf, 8.

5. "State of Allyship-In-Action Benchmark Study," 8.

6. Kaitlin Woolley and Ayelet Fishbach, "Motivating Personal Growth by Seeking Discomfort," *Psychological Science* 33, no. 4 (April 2022): 510–23, https://doi.org/10.1177/09567976211044685.

7. Lyra, "The State of Workforce Mental Health in 2022," https://www.lyrahealth.com/resources/white-paper/2022-state-of-workforce-mental-health-report.

8. The Centre for Global Inclusion, "About GDEIB," https://centreforglobalinclusion.org/what-we-do/the-gdeib/about-gdeib.html.

9. For a resource applying Kurt Lewin's Change Theory to the business context, see Gilmore Crosby, *Planned Change: Why Kurt Lewin's Social Science Is Still Best Practice for Business Results, Change Management, and Human Progress*, 1st ed. (New York: Productivity Press, 2020), https://doi. org/10.4324/9781003082491.

Step 1: Decide This Can't Wait

1. Drew Goldstein et al., "Unlocking the Potential of Chief Diversity Officers," McKinsey and Company, November 18, 2022, https://www.mckinsey.com/capabilities/people-and-organizational-performance/our-insights/unlocking-the-potential-of-chief-diversity-officers.

2. Brian Good, "Hiring of Chief Diversity Officers Triples Over Past Sixteen Months but Representation in the Workforce Is Still Lagging," Fair360.com, March 15, 2021, https://www.diversityinc.com/hiring-of-chief-diversity-officers-triples-over-past-16-months-but-representation-in-the-workforce-is-still-lagging-2.

3. Russell Reynolds, "A Global Look at the Chief Diversity Officer Landscape," April 21, 2023, https://www.russellreynolds.com/en/insights/reports-surveys/a-global-look-at-the-chief-diversity-officer-landscape.

4. P. Christopher Early and Soon Ang, *Cultural Intelligence: Individual Interactions Across Cultures* (Redwood City, CA: Stanford Business Books, 2003).

5. Alex P. Lindsey et al., "The Impact of Method, Motivation, and Empathy on Diversity Training Effectiveness," *Journal of Business and Psychology* 30, no. 3 (November 2014): 605–17, https://doi.org/10.1007/s10869-014-9384-3.

6. iCIMS, "How to Recruit and Hire Gen Z: Class of Covid-19," https://www.icims.com/class-of-covid-19/#get-report.

7. Olivia Konotey-Ahulu, "Gen Z's Desire for DEI Clashes With Reality of Culture Wars," Bloomberg, September 6, 2023, https://www.bloomberg.com/news/articles/2023-09-06/gen-z-s-desire-for-dei-focus-clashes-with-reality-of-culture-wars.

8. john a. powell, Stephen Menendian, and Wendy Ake, "Targeted Universalism: Policy and Practice," Othering and Belonging Institute, May 2019, https://belonging.berkeley.edu/targeted-universalism.

9. Adam D. Galinsky and Gordon B. Moskowitz, "Perspective-Taking: Decreasing Stereotype Expression, Stereotype Accessibility, and In-Group Favoritism," *Journal of Personality and Social Psychology* 78, no. 4 (2000): 708–24, https://doi.org/10.1037/0022-3514.78.4.708.

10. Affirm, "Employee Listening and DEI," LinkedIn.com, February 28, 2022, https://www.linkedin.com/pulse/employee-listening-dei-affirm.

11. Office of Personnel Management, "Government-Wide DEIA: Our Progress and Path Forward to Building a Better Workforce for the American People," 2022, https://www.opm.gov/policy-data-oversight/diversity-equity-inclusion-and-accessibility/reports/DEIA-Annual-Report-2022.pdf.

12. Carly Knight, Frank Dobbin, and Alexandra Kalev, "Under the Radar: Visibility and the Effects of Discrimination Lawsuits in Small and Large Firms," *American Sociological Review* 87, no. 2 (April 2022): 175–201, https://doi.org/10.1177/00031224221077677.

13. Kevin S. Groves and Ann E. Feyerherm, "Leader Cultural Intelligence in Context: Testing the Moderate Effects of Team Cultural Diversity on Leader and Team Performance," *Group and Organization Management* 36, no. 5 (October 2011): 535–66, https://doi.org/10.1177/1059601111415664; and David Livermore, *Leading With Cultural Intelligence: The Real Secret to Success*, 2nd ed. (New York: AMACOM, 2015).

14. Michelle MiJung Kim, *The Wake Up: Closing the Gap Between Good Intentions and Real Change* (New York: Hachette Go, 2021).

15. Loretta J. Ross, "Don't Call People Out—Call Them In," TED video, 14:18, https://youtu.be/xw_720iQDss.

STEP 2: BUILD YOUR TRIBE

1. Evelyn R. Carter and Natalie Johnson, "To Sustain DEI Momentum, Companies Must Invest in Three Areas," *Harvard Business Review*, November 4, 2022, https://hbr.org/2022/11/to-sustain-dei-momentum-companies-must-invest-in-3-areas.

2. Carter and Johnson, "To Sustain DEI Momentum."

STEP 3: MAP THE ROUTE

1. Malia Wollan, "How to Navigate a Maze," *New York Times*, October 17, 2018, https://www.nytimes.com/2018/10/17/magazine/how-to-navigate-a-maze.html.

2. Indeed.com, "Diversity, Equity, Inclusion, and Belonging (DEIB)," https://www.indeed.com/esg/deib.

3. Nike.com, "Diversity, Equity, and Inclusion," https://about.nike.com/en/impact/focus-areas/diversity-equity-inclusion.

4. Delta.com, "Diversity, Equity, and Inclusion: Lifting as We Climb," https://www.delta.com/us/en/about-delta/diversity.

5. Uber.com, "Diversity, Equity, and Inclusion," https://www.uber.com/us/en/about/diversity/.

6. Rakesh Kochhar, "The Enduring Grip of the Gender Pay Gap," Pew Research Center, March 1, 2023, https://www.pewresearch.org/social-trends/2023/03/01/the-enduring-grip-of-the-gender-pay-gap/.

7. Google, "2022 Diversity Annual Report," https://about.google/belonging/diversity-annual-report/2022.

STEP 4: SHARE YOUR DEI PLAN

1. John Kotter, *Leading Change* (Boston: Harvard Business Review Press, 2012), 87.

STEP 5: EQUIP SUPERHEROES

1. Edward H. Chang et al., "The Mixed Effects of Online Diversity Training," *PNAS* 116, no. 16 (April 1, 2019): 7778–83, https://doi.org/10.1073/pnas.1816076116.

2. Dove and CROWN Coalition, "CROWN Act Research Studies," 2023, https://www.thecrownact.com/research-studies.

3. CROWN Coalition, "Help Us End Hair Discrimination in the Workplace, Schools, and Pools," posted on Organize For, https://campaigns.organizefor.org/petitions/help-make-hair-discrimination-illegal.

4. Vinita Mehta, "Are People With Tattoos Stigmatized?," *Psychology Today*, September 28, 2018, https://www.psychologytoday.com/us/blog/head-games/201809/are-people-tattoos-stigmatized.

5. Christine E. Wormuth, "Army Directive 2022-09 (Soldier Tattoos)," Secretary of the Army for the Department of Defense, June 22, 2022, https://armypubs.army.mil/epubs/DR_pubs/DR_a/ARN35733-ARMY_DIR_2022-09-000-WEB-1.pdf.

6. W. Edwards Deming, *Out of the Crisis*, first MIT Press ed. (Cambridge, MA: MIT Press, 2000), 315.

7. Vivian Hunt et al., "Diversity Wins: How Inclusion Matters," McKinsey and Company, May 2020, https://www.mckinsey.com/~/media/mckinsey/

featured%20insights/diversity%20and%20inclusion/
diversity%20wins%20how%20inclusion%20matters/
diversity-wins-how-inclusion-matters-vf.pdf.

8. Henrik Bresman and Amy C. Edmonson, "Research:
To Excel, Diverse Teams Need Psychological Safety,"
Harvard Business Review, March 17, 2022, https://
hbr.org/2022/03/research-to-excel-diverse-teams-
need-psychological-safety.

9. See Amy C. Edmonson, *The Fearless Organization:
Creating Psychological Safety in the Workplace for
Learning, Innovation, and Growth* (Hoboken, NJ:
Wiley, 2018).

10. Jodi-Ann Burey, "The Myth of Bringing Your Full,
Authentic Self to Work," TedX Seattle, November
2020, https://www.ted.com/talks/jodi_ann_burey_
the_myth_of_bringing_your_full_authentic_self_to_
work/transcript.

11. Mary Baker and Teresa Zuech, "Gartner HR
Research Finds 68% of Employees Would Consider
Leaving Their Employer for an Organization That
Takes a Stronger Stance on Societal and Cultural
Issues," Gartner, March 3, 2021, https://www.
gartner.com/en/newsroom/press-releases/2021-03-
04-gartner-hr-research-finds-sixty-eight-percent-of-
employees-would-consider-leaving-their-employer-
for-an-organization-that-takes-a-stronger-stance-on-
societal-and-cultural-issues.

STEP 6: PLAN DEI VICTORIES

1. Teresa M. Amabile and Steven J. Kramer, "The Power of Small Wins," *Harvard Business Review*, May 2011, https://hbr.org/2011/05/the-power-of-small-wins.

2. Sarah Bloznalis, "Sixteen Employee Recognition Examples to Boost Engagement and Satisfaction," Workhuman, March 22, 2023, https://www.workhuman.com/blog/employee-recognition-examples.

STEP 7: USE THE SNOWBALL EFFECT

1. I. E. Dror et al., "Letter to the Editor: The Bias Snowball and the Bias Cascade Effects: Two Distinct Biases That May Impact Forensic Decision Making," *Journal of Forensic Sciences* (2017): doi: 10.1111/1556-4029.13496. https://www.bondsolon.com/media/166089/dror_jfs_cascade_vs_snowball_biaspdf.pdf

2. Daniel Kahneman, *Thinking, Fast and Slow* (New York: Farrar, Straus, and Giroux, 2013).

3. Meredith Leigh Moore, "Five Keys to Recruiting and Retaining Women in STEM," YouTube video, 54:27, https://www.youtube.com/watch?v=2WAB52w_4TY.

4. Michael Hyatt and Megan Hyatt Miller, "Episode: *Get the Feedback You Need to Grow*," Business Accelerator, June 7, 2022, https://businessaccelerator.com/get-the-feedback-you-need-to-grow/?transcript.

Step 8: Make DEI Last

1. James O'Toole, *Leading Change: The Argument for Values-Based Leadership* (New York: Ballantine, 1996), 72.

2. Robert Rodriguez, *Employee Resource Group Excellence: Grow High Performing ERGs to Enhance Diversity, Equality, Belonging, and Business Impact* (Hoboken, NJ: Wiley, 2022).

Bonus Step: Handling Resistors

1. Eric Shuman, Eric Knowles, and Amit Goldenberg, "To Overcome Resistance to DEI, Understand What's Driving It," *Harvard Business Review*, March 1, 2023, https://hbr.org/2023/03/to-overcome-resistance-to-dei-understand-whats-driving-it.

2. Sandra Upton, "Fact or Myth: We Can't Find Diverse Candidates for Our Team," Cultural Intelligence Center, February 14, 2019, https://culturalq.com/blog/fact-or-myth-we-cant-find-diverse-candidates-for-our-team.

Conclusion: Your DEI Roadmap

3. Rohini Anand, *Leading Global Diversity, Equity, and Inclusion: A Guide for Systemic Change in Multinational Organizations* (Oakland, CA: Berrett-Koehler, 2022), 23.

Acknowledgments

THERE ARE SO many people to thank. However, it is not hard to know where to start. My husband, Robert, has always been my biggest ally, both in my work and personal life. His support throughout this process has been unwavering. Without it, along with the overwhelming support from our two amazing adult children, Alexis and Devin, I'm confident that the hard work would have felt ten times harder.

My amazing mother, Mattie Pearl Veal, is one of the most caring and dependable people anyone could ever meet. As a single mom, she did a phenomenal job raising me. There is no way I would have achieved so many things in my life and career, including completing this book, without the values she instilled in me and the support she has provided my entire life.

A huge thank you to the Embolden Media Group team and especially my amazing writing coach, Danielle Butler. I could not have written this book without you. Danielle, your tireless guidance, encouragement, and patience helped me manage the roller coaster of emotions I felt during this process. You, along with everyone who allocated time to review drafts of the manuscript and provide incredibly valuable input, helped me get to the finish line.

I'm also grateful for those individuals who have supported me and my work over the years. My colleague and friend, Dr. David Livermore, has been pushing me to write a book for years. I finally did it. Another huge supporter has been the brilliant Dr. Barbara Nobles Crawford. I met Dr. Crawford when doing consulting work for Harvard University. She was one of the leading in-house organization behavior and development consultants at the university. Since that time, you have mentored, supported, and inspired me in more ways than I can count. You are my shero.

Lastly, I want to thank A. James Heynen. We met when I was a young twenty-three-year-old college graduate with very little professional work experience, but you saw something great in me and hired me as a consultant with your management consulting firm. In the world of DEI, we would say you were my first executive sponsor. You modeled what real allyship looks like. That early opportunity put my career on an amazing trajectory. And only God knew that over thirty years later our lives would cross again, and you would, once again, become one of my biggest allies.

ABOUT THE AUTHOR

D R. SANDRA UPTON (she/her) is a sought-after DEI and organizational development thought leader who works with DEI professionals and organizations around the globe. Using a research-based, change-management framework and culturally intelligent strategies, Sandra uses her decades of experience in this space to support organizations' efforts to create behaviors and systems that support diverse, equitable, inclusive, and culturally intelligent work environments.

Prior to relaunching her own consulting practice, Dr. Upton was vice president, global diversity practice with the Cultural Intelligence Center and was responsible for providing strategic leadership and expertise on diversity, equity, and inclusion matters for numerous clients across the globe. She led organizational responses to the growing demand from global and Fortune 500 companies to Ivy League universities. She is a frequent speaker, has written numerous articles and blogs on DEI, has been featured on several global podcasts and has worked across numerous countries and continents.

Upton Consulting Group

Choose courage over comfort on your DEI journey with UCG's products and services.

+ DEI Propel Course

+ Keynotes

+ Consulting

+ Coaching

+ Training

Printed in the USA
CPSIA information can be obtained
at www.ICGtesting.com
LVHW051437180224
772154LV00021B/213/J